DISCONNECTED

THOMAS KERSTING

DISCONNECTED

HOW TO RECONNECT OUR DIGITALLY DISTRACTED KIDS

CONTENTS

INTRODUCTION

I was a helmet-less, Big-Wheel-riding child of the 1980s. I walked a half-mile in the dark to the bus stop each morning, got bullied sometimes, threw eggs at other kids on Halloween, and rode my Huffy all around town when I was ten. I played tackle football with no pads and baseball without a heart protector. I sat in the back seat of my mom's Ford Granada without wearing a seatbelt. I was outside all day long in the summer along with the other kids in my neighborhood. Nothing was planned out for us and the only thing we cared about was having fun and being adventurous. We had Ataris and Nintendos but spent much less time playing them than we did playing outside with each other. Handheld devices did not exist, so my friends and I were never distracted from the fun we had together. When it was time for dinner, we were home on time and ate with our families—every night. We had little worries and were just, well, kids. And we all survived.

Today, my greatest source of pride is being a father. It is the most rewarding thing in the world but also the most frightening as the world that I once lived in as a child is much different from the one my children live in today. In many ways this is a good thing. We have made great strides. My kids always wear their seatbelts, never get on their bikes without a helmet, and do not throw eggs at other kids on Halloween. The dangers you and I faced as children pale in comparison to the one our kids are facing. This is a danger that is changing the very meaning of what it means to be a kid and even what it means to be a human—a danger that is wounding our children's mental, emotional, and social health like nothing we've seen before.

A couple of years ago my family and I had enjoyed a wonderful trip out West. We visited a number of National Parks including Yellowstone, Bryce Canyon, and Zion. It was the vacation of a lifetime. The flight back home to LaGuardia Airport in New York was long, and I remember feeling eager to exit the plane, get to the baggage claim area, and arrive home. When we finally disembarked the plane and started making our way through the terminal I was stopped in my tracks. I felt like I had just entered the twilight zone. Screens were everywhere, and not just in the palms of the people I passed. Flashing tablets loaded with social media apps and games, installed by the airport, were perfectly positioned in front of every bar stool and restaurant seat. The first thing that came to mind was the many people I had met from all around the world and the many things I had learned while sipping a beer from one of those stools. The airport had taken all of that away and replaced these experiences with machines. At the time, I had been speaking for several years to parent groups about the negative effect that too much technology was having on our children's well-being, so I was ahead of the curve, but this experience was different—this was technology on steroids.

As my wife and kids and I continued our long walk to the baggage claim area I felt helpless in a way. I hoped that what I had witnessed was an isolated case, limited to the terminal I had flown into, but it wasn't. As we walked past more restaurants, bars and waiting areas, the scene was the same—nearly everyone was connected to a screen and disconnected from each other. Strangers remained strangers. Although I was reaching a lot of people through my lectures, counseling sessions, and television appearances, I knew I had to do more and that is why I wrote this book.

What you will find in the coming pages is a call to action. The cold hard fact is this: we and our children do not have control over electronic devices and screens; electronic devices and screens have control over us. Much of what you will read in the coming pages is fascinating and also frightening, but if you stick with me you will see that there is plenty of light at the end of the tunnel. I'll share with you real life stories from my experiences as a private practice therapist and public school counselor. I've also included lots of scientific evidence and research-based studies to support my claims. You will discover how the modern-day machines, the screens, are the cause of many of our children's problems, ranging from anxiety disorders to family problems to school and social problems. Unplugging our children and ourselves will not be easy, but if you follow my advice it will be possible. In the final chapter of the book I provide a host of tips and strategies that will help you to pull your children, and yourselves, away from the screens and closer to each other.

PART ONE

The Impact of Electronic Devices on Kids' Brains

CHAPTER 1

Acquired Attention Deficit Disorder

From 2002 until today I've been a member of the Intervention & Referral Services Committee (I&RS) at a local high school where I work as a counselor. The role of the committee is to provide academic accommodations to students with temporary or permanent disabilities as long as there is evidence that the disability is affecting the student's learning. Some common disabilities my committee has reviewed over the years include concussions, diabetes, Crohn's disease, and specific learning issues.

During the 2009 school year the types of disabilities referred to my committee started to change. We began receiving countless referrals for teenage students diagnosed with Attention Deficit Hyperactivity Disorder. Attention Deficit Hyperactivity Disorder, also known as ADHD, is a neurological condition that causes a combination of the following symptoms: inattention; disorganization and lack of focus; and sometimes impulsivity and hyperactivity. These symptoms are very noticeable by age five, and the average age at diagnosis is eight years old. Strangely, my committee was receiving dozens of referrals for fourteen- and fifteen-year-olds newly diagnosed with the disorder.

As a school counselor by day and private practice therapist by night, I have more than twenty years of experience working with ADHD children and their families, and this influx of attention deficit teenagers wasn't making sense to me. Was it possible that so many parents and teachers had overlooked the symptoms when these kids were in elementary or middle school? Could this many children possibly have slipped through the cracks, I wondered? Something wasn't adding up.

I started to aggressively research this new ADHD phenomenon and even consulted with neighboring school districts. My colleagues saw precisely what I was seeing—an inordinate number of teenagers being diagnosed with ADHD. My research led me to the work of Dr. Gary Small, professor of psychiatry and Director of the UCLA Longevity Center at the Semel Institute for Neuroscience and Human Behavior. Dr. Small is one of the world's top innovators in science and technology. In 2007 Small began researching technology's impact on the brain and discovered that when research subjects spent as little as an hour a day online, the activity patterns in their brains changed dramatically.[1] According to Small, "the human brain is malleable, always changing in response to its environment." Dr. Small explains that the brain is very sensitive. Every stimulation the brain receives causes a complex cascade of neurochemical electrical consequences. With repeated stimuli the neural circuits in the brain become excited and if other neural circuits are neglected they will be weakened. A young person's brain, which is still developing, is particularly sensitive and is also the kind of brain that is most exposed to modern technology.

Dr. Small discovered that because kids of this generation spend so much time using powerful electronic devices, their brains were changing, something known as *neuroplasticity*. Neuroplasticity is the brain's ability to reorganize itself by forming new neural connections, leaving behind past traits and developing new ones. Could all of this "screen time" be changing kids' brains, thereby causing older children to display inattentiveness, lack of focus, and disorganization—all symptoms of ADHD? According to Dr. Elias Aboujaoude, director of Stanford University's Impulse Control Disorders Clinic, "the more we become used to just sound bites and tweets, the less patient we will become with more complex, more meaningful information. And I do think we might lose the ability to analyze things with any depth and nuance. Like any skill, if you don't use it you lose it."[2] This technology use and brain neuroplasticity research prompted Dr. John Ratey, Clinical Professor of Psychiatry at Harvard Medical School, to coin the term *acquired attention deficit disorder*, describing how too much screen time was rewiring kids' brains. This *acquired attention deficit* term fascinated me because it meant that potentially thousands of teenagers were being misdiagnosed with a disorder they didn't have and were even being prescribed powerful medication to treat it. I decided to dig deeper with my caseload of recently diagnosed ADHD students at the high school. I gathered records and notes from their elementary and middle school counselors and teachers and, as I had suspected, I could find no evidence of ADHD symptoms at earlier stages in their education.

Although Dr. Small's research was too new to be conclusive, he believed that in addition to attention deficit symptoms, too much time online might cause a host of other issues from problems maintaining eye contact to difficulty interacting with others. Following Small's groundbreaking research, more studies have come out, linking excessive online use to anxiety, depression, and behavioral issues. The most recent, conducted by Dr. Michael Van Ameringen, evaluated 254 freshmen at McMaster University in Ontario, Canada. Thirty-three of the students met criteria for internet addiction while 107 met the criteria for problematic internet use. The students' mental health was also assessed during the study and those who met the criteria for internet addiction showed higher rates of inattention, impulsivity, anxiety, and depression.[3]

If you've ever seen an image of the human brain, you've likely noticed those electrical impulses that resemble tree branches extending from the outer wall of the brain. These tree branches are known as *neuropathways*, and they play an important role in human functionality. Each neuropathway is responsible for how we communicate, cope, focus, concentrate, and socialize, just to name a few crucial functions of the brain. For example, if you've ever taken away your child's video game console or smartphone, the way in which he copes with this punishment may have a lot to do with how his brain is wired. A child with healthy coping and emotional skills will naturally become upset or disappointed by the punishment, while a child with unhealthy coping and emotional skills may go into a fit of rage. And it seems that more and more children are displaying the latter.

— § —

It takes a lot for a brain to change its wiring—typically three or more hours per day of consistent stimulating activity. Three hours per day might sound like a lot of stimulation, but it's not. According to a recent survey conducted by CNN, the typical thirteen-year-old spends a lot more than three hours per day engaged in highly stimulating brain activities.[4] Try eight or more hours per day, on average, seven days a week, staring at the bright lights of smartphones, tablets, and computer screens. The result: a new brain. A brain that is lit up like a Christmas tree; a brain that has literally grown new branches in order to adapt to its new environment, cyberspace; a brain that is hyper-focused on tweets, posts, and likes and not very focused on Mrs. Smith's classroom lectures; a brain that is brilliant at communicating through texts and posts but struggles with face-to-face communication. Frightening!

A December 2015 study in the *Journal of Clinical Psychiatry* found that ADHD diagnoses soared 43 percent in the United States in the first decade of this century, with more than one in ten youths now diagnosed with the disorder. The number of teenagers diagnosed with ADHD rose 52 percent between 2003 and 2015. And while ADHD is traditionally more common in boys than girls, the study also found a 55-percent increase in girls being diagnosed with the disorder.[5] The study was not designed to look for the underlying reasons for the changes, but it referred to past studies, suggesting that the rise may be attributed to special-education policy or increased public awareness, which I disagree with. I believe the increase in ADHD diagnoses has everything to do with the amount of time children are spending in front of screens.

When I first discovered all of this ADHD and neuroplasticity research back in 2009, I felt the need to educate parents, so I began lecturing. I called my lecture "Digitally Distracted: Parenting in the Age of Technology." Schools would hire me to speak in the evening to the parents of their students. While the bulk of my discussions involved brain neuroplasticity and ADHD, I also talked about chronic video game playing, internet surfing, and television watching, and how it was affecting children in other ways. I included a lot of statistics that I'll discuss in the next chapter and warned parents that if they did not get a grip on their children's media diet, as well as their own media diet, that we would see a surge in mental and emotional health disorders in the near future. Although the parents in attendance were fascinated by my lecture and told their friends about it, few of them took the necessary steps to change their children's media habits or their own. Looking back, I don't think they were ready for this radical information. After about a year of lecturing, I stopped. I became occupied with a television series I was hosting and was busy raising my own children. But I could not stop thinking about the problems that digital media were creating, and these problems seemed to get worse as the next several years unfolded.

Fast-forward to 2016, and the future problems that I had predicted during my 2009 lectures are now upon us. More and more kids are becoming emotionally fragile and lack critical coping skills because they are not spending enough time engaged in the real world, person to person. No matter where you go, whether it's the beach or a ball game, it seems that everyone is disconnected from one another and connected to a device instead. Our heads are buried in our tablets and smartphones, and face-to-face communication is slowly becoming a thing of the past. This lack of face-to-face interaction, particularly for children, is evident in their reduced social and communication skills, making it difficult for them to handle the everyday bumps in the road of life. The end result: a substantial increase in stress, anxiety, and self-esteem issues.

Although my I&RS Committee still receives referrals for students who are misdiagnosed with ADHD, during the last couple of years the pendulum has swung; a whole new set of disabilities has emerged—anxiety disorders. Anxiety is now the number one type of disability that my I&RS committee reviews. And at my private counseling practice, I have received more referrals for middle-school-aged children with major anxiety disorders in the last year than I'd received in the previous sixteen years combined. Do I think this has something to do with too much screen time? You better believe I do.

I want you to imagine the life of a typical sixteen-year-old girl for a moment. Let's call her Sarah. Sarah's mom enters her room each morning to wake her for school because Sarah somehow slept through the buzz of her alarm clock even though it woke up the neighbors. Sarah likely got little sleep the night before because she couldn't pull herself away from the endless group chat she was a part of. After her mom's third or fourth attempt to wake her, Sarah finally emerges from her deep sleep, yells at her mom, and reluctantly gets on her feet. Sarah's first instinct, before she has even realized she's awake, is to reach for her phone, which is on her nightstand within arm's reach. She proceeds to brush her teeth, change into her clothing, and eat breakfast as she catches up on the text messages and social media gossip left over from the night before. Finally, Sarah's mother is able to hurry her into the car in an effort to prevent her from being late to school. During the short commute, Sarah moves her thumbs vigorously across the screen of her smartphone, completely oblivious to the world around her, including her mom. By the time her mom has reached the drop-off point, Sarah has already sent and received dozens of text messages since the time she got out of bed. As Sarah exits the car and walks towards the entrance of her school, her head is down, her eyes are fixated on her smartphone, and her thumbs are texting away. She never said thank you or good-bye to her mom. She is too distracted.

Unfortunately, this is an accurate portrayal of many modern-day kids. And because all of this is so new to us parents, we struggle with strategies to handle this behavior, thinking it is just a sign of the times. We simply don't know any better. Even more concerning is that for millions of boys and girls around the world like Sarah, this type of inappropriate behavior isn't just an occasional thing, it's an everyday thing. Many kids spend nearly every waking second of every day, seven days a week, glued to an electronic device, completely oblivious to life on Earth. Their brains become disconnected from the world around them, making it difficult to handle real-life events and adversities.

Yes, neuroplasticity is real and can have negative consequences, but even more concerning is something known as *neural pruning*. Neural pruning is a natural and normal occurrence during adolescence, and it is the brain's way of weeding out pathways that are used less often. If you've seen the movie *Inside Out* you'll recognize neural pruning as the process that occurs as eleven-year-old Riley tries to assimilate her family's move to a new city. Joy and the other emotions inside her brain fight against this neural pruning but finally accept it as part of the maturing process. But these changes in the brain aren't always positive. For example, if young folks spend most of their time communicating through text messaging rather than face-to-face, the brain will weed out the neural pathways that are necessary for becoming a good face-to-face communicator.

Although more research needs to be done to be conclusive, perhaps the changes that occur in the brain from spending too much time for too many years staring into a screen explain why many young folks are struggling with simple skills such as having a conversation with a stranger or interviewing for a job. I've spoken with many job recruiters who've told me that when they interview recent college graduates, it seems as if something is missing. Job candidates lack charisma and display poor social skills. Sitting through a face-to-face interview seems very unnatural to them. I see this too at my private counseling practice. Many of the young folks I work with struggle to make eye contact while communicating or become anxious while participating in social engagements or group interactions. More and more parents that I speak with tell me that their child struggles to form friendships and is rarely invited to friends' homes or have friends over at their home. Perhaps this growing crop of antisocial kids is the result of neural pruning? Ask yourself this question: if the neuropathways that are responsible for producing strong social skills have been severed, how is it possible to be, well, social?

Another issue I'm seeing on a daily basis with kids is poor coping skills. Over the last couple of years there have been an unprecedented number of meltdowns in my office because of a C on an exam or a mean social media remark. Could this loss of coping skills have something to do with neural pruning? I think so. The bottom line is this: more kids than ever before are struggling to communicate, socialize, or cope effectively with real-life matters because they are not living in the real world. I believe a short-circuiting effect has occurred in their brains, sending their emotions into a tailspin and creating a host of different mental and emotional disorders.

When I was a graduate student in the late 1990s, I took a course called "The Biopsychosocial Perspectives of Drugs." The professor, Dr. Hamaerle, told us the following story about how addiction can change brain functionality.

> One night a forty-five-year-old man was pulled over by a police officer for having a broken taillight. When he rolled down the window and handed the officer his license and registration, the officer noticed an overwhelming smell of alcohol coming from his car and asked him if he had been drinking. The man responded that he had not. Although the man wasn't slurring his words and showed no signs of intoxication, the officer asked him to step out of the car because he couldn't get past the strong smell of alcohol. The officer conducted the appropriate field sobriety tests, which the man passed with flying colors. He showed no signs of intoxication whatsoever. The officer still could not dismiss the smell of alcohol permeating the air, so he brought the man to the station to conduct a Breathalyzer exam just to be certain.
>
> At the time, the legal blood alcohol content (BAC) was .10 and anyone with a .10 or higher would be charged with a DWI. Keep in mind that for an average person a BAC of .20 would render them extremely intoxicated, a .30 would likely result in a coma, and a .40 would usually mean death. This man's BAC reading was .62. Astounding!
>
> So how is it that this man was even alive, let alone displaying zero signs of intoxication? The following day when the man was sober, he was released from his jail cell; it was at that point that he started displaying the classic signs of intoxication, including slurred speech, body tremors, and an inability to walk straight.

This story is an example of how powerful the human brain is. Because the man was a seasoned alcoholic who drank excessively every day, his brain adapted to its new normal—being intoxicated. Sobriety was foreign to his brain and intoxication was normal. The story of the alcoholic is similar to my experiences with many of the children and teenagers I counsel. Because cyberspace is where they spend the majority of their time, their brains have adapted to this new environment, rendering the real world a foreign place to them. Unfortunately, when some of these youngsters reach adulthood they will end up like a former client of mine, whom I'll call Jan.[6]

Jan was a twenty-four-year-old millennial whom I began seeing at my private counseling practice to help her with anxiety. I could feel her anxiety the moment I met her; she was an emotional wreck. Jan explained to me that she was always anxious and just couldn't shake the constant, uncomfortable feeling. She needed help. Although she was a college graduate, she worked part time in a non-challenging job because it was safe for her; her anxiety prevented her from going out into the world and pursuing the kind of career that her college degree would allow. As I got to know Jan I started to explore her technology use. I asked her to describe for me her normal routine when she got home from work each evening. She told me that she would typically log on to her computer, scroll around on her smartphone, and watch television. I gave her a two-part daily assignment that I wanted her to try between sessions. First, I wanted her to track her feelings when she was using an electronic device to see if she felt any of the anxiety during those times. Next, I wanted her to sit in total silence every day for fifteen minutes, without any distractions present, including electronic devices. She explained to me that she had never done anything like this before but she agreed to give it a try.

When Jan returned the following week she told me that she did not experience any anxiety while using her electronic devices, which is what I had expected. During her fifteen-minute meditations, however, while she was disconnected from electronics, she experienced extreme panic and anxiety and was only able to do the assignment twice. I concluded that because Jan was constantly connected to the cyberworld, the real world had turned into a frightening, foreign place for her. It makes sense when you think about it. Look at it like this: what would happen to a lion if it were released into the wild after having lived its entire life in a cage? The lion would not survive because the lion's natural habitat would now be the cage, not the wilderness. The wilderness would seem foreign to the lion. Jan was no different. She functioned just fine in her cyberworld but not in her real world. It would take a lot of work to get her brain to readapt to the real world. In the final chapter I will teach you these strategies.

Unfortunately, many of the younger people I counsel are the future Jans. As I mentioned earlier, not a day goes by that I'm not calming down a high school student having an emotional breakdown over something trivial. In chapter 3 I'll discuss what it takes for your child to strengthen their emotional intelligence and how you can help them. But for now I will leave you with a few examples of some teenagers that I counseled in the days just before writing this chapter.

I received a phone call from a distressed parent whose teenage son needed to be cleared for suicidal ideation before he could return to school. Luckily, I was able to get the family in for an appointment that night. They seemed like a really well rounded, good family, yet the boy was emotionally distraught. Here is what transpired: the boy's father found inappropriate content on the boy's phone and took the phone away from him as a punishment. The next morning, the parents found a lengthy note from the boy that resembled a suicide note. The boy felt that he could not go on living without his phone as he would "have no life," no friends.

Next I received a call from a very concerned mom about her daughter. Her daughter had an emotional breakdown because she discovered on social media that her best friend was getting together with another girl; she was afraid her best friend was going to drop her. As my conversation progressed with the mother, she told me she had read some material that her daughter had secretly written. The girl expressed that she felt unpopular, ugly, uncomfortable around people and that she wished she would die. When I asked the mom about her daughter's social media use, the mom told me that her daughter was on social media and her smartphone 24/7.

Next, a coach friend of mine told me a story about something that had happened to her over the weekend. Her team had taken an overnight trip to Connecticut, and the owner of the facility where they stayed and played their games had a rule: no cellphones allowed during the entire trip. The owner felt that they were a distraction to the players and affected team camaraderie. A parent of one of the players threatened to sue the owner because he felt his rights were violated by not being allowed to contact his daughter on her phone if there was an emergency. I wonder if this man's daughter struggles with fear and worry?

Before we move on to the next chapter, I want to share one last story. I recently accompanied my nine-year-old daughter's class on a field trip to a raptor hospital. The instructor showed the class a beautiful barn owl that had been injured when it was young. The children loved it. The barn owl had lived at the facility for a number of years and was very accustomed to humans. One of the children asked the facilitator why the owl had not been released back into the wild. The facilitator explained that although the owl's injury had healed, the owl would die if it were released into the wild because it would not know how to hunt for prey and would therefore starve. Essentially, the owl would not know how to survive in its "natural habitat."

Our children aren't much different from the barn owl or the lion. No, their electronic devices aren't going to kill them, but we need to make sure that our children are developing in their natural habitat, the physical world around them. Children are meant to be playing outside with other children, getting dirty and scraping their knees.

Their imaginations beg them to stare at the sky and make shapes out of clouds. That is what they were born to do. So let's make sure that they spend less time indoors staring at screens and more time outdoors staring at the sky.

CHAPTER 2

Cyberspace Children: A Full-Time Job

In 2005, the Kaiser Family Foundation released the findings from a 2004 study of children's media use. The study tracked trends in the amount and types of electronic media that kids used. Their findings revealed that the average eight- to eighteen-year-old spent six-and-a-half hours per day using electronic media.[7] The researchers intended to conduct the study every four years but when 2008 came around, they were hesitant because they felt they had reached a ceiling on the amount of time kids could spend in front of machines. They didn't think it was possible for kids to spend more time using electronic media than the previous study had revealed. They believed there just wasn't enough time in the day for the number to increase. They conducted the study again anyway in 2008 and were stunned by the outcome. The amount of time children were using electronic media had risen by over an hour, to seven hours and thirty-eight minutes per day, seven days a week.[8] The average kid in America was spending more time per week plugged in to electronic devices than the average full-time worker was spending at work. In fact, kids were spending more time using electronic devices than doing any other activity including sleep. Two changes occurred between 2004 and 2008 that led to this increase: YouTube and Facebook. Social media was born.

The Kaiser study conducted in 2008 tracked four specific types of media: television, portable music listening devices, computers, and video games. Below is the 2008 breakdown.

TELEVISION

- The average eight- to eighteen-year-old spent four-and-a-half hours per day watching TV

- 99 percent of households had at least one television

- 80 percent of homes had three televisions

- 71 percent of all eight- to eighteen-year-olds had a television in their bedroom; these kids spent an hour more per day watching television

- 50 percent of eleven- to fourteen-year-olds had no television-watching rules

- 75 percent of fifteen- to eighteen-year-olds had no television-watching rules

- 64 percent of households left the television on during dinner

- By age eighteen, the average adolescent will have seen 200,000 acts of violence on television

COMPUTERS

- The amount of time spent using computers increased by 50 percent from 2004 to 2008

- The three most popular computer activities were **social networking sites, computer games, and YouTube**

- 62 percent of kids claimed that they lie to their parents about what they look at on the web

- 53 percent deleted their browsing history so parents couldn't discover what they've been up to

- 75 percent of seventh to twelfth graders had created a profile on a social media site

- The average eleven- to fourteen-year-old spent 1:07 hours per day on Facebook

VIDEO GAMES

- 50 percent of kids had a video game system in their bedroom
- 52 percent of all video games were played on handheld devices
- Those who did play video games spent two hours a day doing so
- 25 percent of eight- to ten-year-olds played violent video games
- 60 percent of eleven- to fourteen-year-olds played violent video games
- 72 percent of fifteen- to eighteen-year-olds played violent video games

MUSIC DEVICES

- Listening to music was the second most popular media activity among eight- to eighteen-year-olds
- Eight- to ten-year-olds spent 1:08 hours per day listening to music
- Eleven- to fourteen-year-olds spent 2:22 hours per day listening to music
- Fifteen- to eighteen-year-olds spent 3:03 hours per day listening to music

The Kaiser Study also concluded that by age twenty-one this generation will have:

- Played more than 10,000 hours of video games

- Sent and received 250,000 emails and text

- Spent 10,000 hours on phones

- Watched more than 20,000 hours of TV

- Seen more than 500,000 commercials

Although these statistics are alarming, what's even more alarming is that **the Kaiser study did not include smartphone or tablet use** because they weren't relevant in 2008. Today, no matter where you go, the majority of people are walking around with a smartphone in hand, a device that fits in your palm and allows access to just about every form of media. So if kids were spending seven hours and thirty-eight minutes per day with electronic media back in 2008, how much time are they spending now?

In October of 2015, Common Sense Media conducted the most up-to-date, large-scale, probability-based survey to explore young people's media diets. The findings were that the average American teenager now spends nine hours per day, or sixty-three hours per week, immersed in electronic media, not including school-related technology. Individuals in the study who were labeled "heavy" users spent an incredible thirteen hours and twenty minutes a day with screen media.[9]

PHYSICAL REALITIES

Remember Sarah, the teenager who was glued to her smartphone the moment she got out of bed? If you were to take a stroll through the hallways of your local high school while kids were switching classes, you would be shocked by the scene. Nearly every student is walking the halls with his head and neck down, headphones in the ears, and eyes fixated on a device. If you made your way over to the cafeteria during a lunch period you'd notice that most of the students are fixated on either a laptop, tablet or phone, and disconnected from one another. Head over to the homes of these kids and the picture would be just as bleak, with very little interaction between family members and plenty of interaction with invisible friends on the receiving end of each text and post. And it goes beyond this. "Virtual reality" has gotten so prevalent that it is causing deaths and injuries. According to a July 14, 2016 article in the *LA Times,* two men fell off the edge of an ocean bluff and had to be rescued by fire-fighters because they were playing the game Pokemon Go, and another player was stabbed in a park in a separate incident.[10] These are just a couple of examples of many reported by police across the nation shortly after the game was released.

A January 2016 headline in the *New York Post* proclaimed, "Many NYC students so tech-oriented they can't even sign their own names." That's right, scores of students in New York City, including the children of some state lawmakers, can't sign their own names because all they know are keypads and screens.[11] This means they will be unable to properly sign checks, credit cards, or contracts someday. Pretty scary! None of us anticipated something this extreme, but it is very real and is just one example of how our children's overindulgence in technology is not only reducing their mental and emotional capacity but also their fine motor skills.

Studies conducted with college students over the past few years have also found that smartphones are making the majority of them hallucinate. That's right—hallucinate. It is called "phantom vibration syndrome." Roughly once every two weeks, the majority of the students who were surveyed experienced a "phantom vibration," or a buzzing sensation in their pocket, even though their phone wasn't vibrating. According to Robert Rosenberger, a professor in the School of Public Policy at Georgia Tech, "The phone actually becomes a part of you, and you become trained to perceive the phone's vibrations as an incoming call or text. When a phone shifts in the pocket, it triggers a muscle spasm in your leg that resembles a phone vibration, even though no one is calling."[12]

Around fifteen years ago, after I bought my first cellphone, I experienced this phenomenon. I kept my cellphone in my pocket on vibrate all the time and occasionally felt it vibrate only to reach into my empty pocket and discover that my phone was on my desk. At first I didn't realize why I was having this sensation and figured it must be a kind of Pavlovian reaction. I even went to a doctor just to make sure there wasn't something wrong with me. I remember asking the doctor if it was possible that the muscles in my leg had learned to experience the vibration from my phone, which was why I was having these spasms. I remember him pausing with a puzzled look on his face saying, "Yes, I guess that is possible." I think he learned something from me that day.

Other research suggests that "selfies" can be dangerous to your health. I'm not referring to the stories of people falling off of cliffs or walking into traffic; I'm talking about legitimate physical health issues. Helena Horton, a journalist writing for the UK newspaper *The Telegraph,* documented a phenomenon called "selfie stomach" experienced by many internet and selfie addicts.[13] Horton refers to a twenty-one-year-old self-proclaimed "selfie addict" named Michelle Gore who contracted a painful condition known as Tietze disease from taking too many selfies. The disorder is caused by putting too much strain on the rib cartilage. Gore was taking approximately 200 selfies per day and even had a waterproof case for her phone so that she could stay connected in the shower. Gore finally decided to unplug after she woke one morning to find herself tangled up in cables from all of her different gadgets.

Another physical abnormality occurring in younger generations is something dubbed "tech neck." If you haven't heard of this condition, picture the sagging skin under the chins and jaws of older people. This latest ailment can be found in people between eighteen and thirty-nine years old and dermatologists blame smartphones and tablets because of the repeated bending of the neck to look at portable device screens. This sagging of the jowls used to be found in people who are in their late middle age, but now a lot of young women are visiting dermatologists for the condition.[14]

Back and neck problems are another concern. A study in *Surgery Technology International* found that heavy portable device use causes back and neck problems. According to Kenneth Hansraj, an author of the study, "As the head tilts forward the forces seen by the neck surges to 27 pounds at 15 degrees, 40 pounds at 30 degrees, 49 pounds at 45 degrees and 60 pounds at 60 degrees." Hansraj warned that chronic screen staring could "deteriorate the back and neck muscles to the point of needing surgery."[15]

Finally, researchers at the Yale School of Medicine and renowned physician Dr. Devra Davis claim that cell phones do in fact cause brain cancer. At a symposium in May of 2016, the Yale researchers and Dr. Davis presented several reports maintaining that the developing brains of young children absorb twice the amount of microwave radiation as adults' brains do. Doctors at the symposium feared that prolonged exposure to radiation during childhood would cause cancer later in life. Researchers say it will be a long time before they know how risky cell phone use really is because cancers like brain tumors take ten to twenty years to take root. Doctors at the symposium also warned that the infant brain, even in the womb, is particularly vulnerable to cell phone radiation. Dr. Davis advises pregnant women to keep the phone away from the abdomen, particularly towards the end of pregnancy.[16]

DISTRACTIBILITY

I recently attended a meeting with some administrators and teachers at my school with regard to some of the student issues we are facing. Everyone agreed that the biggest challenge we face is dealing with the declining mental health of our students. During my meeting, everything we discussed about student academics and mental health problems circled back to technology use. Our conversation prompted the principal to share a story. He explained that on several occasions when he greeted students in the hallway they ignored him. He found this to be quite rude until he realized that they hadn't actually ignored him, but rather they were too distracted by the music playing in their headphones to notice him, and it seems that almost all of the students have a set attached to their ears.

Next, the vice principal shared a story. He had read an article in the local paper about a twenty-seven-year-old man who had been tragically killed by a train. The railroad tracks where the man was killed are in Ramsey, New Jersey, close to where I live. There are two sets of tracks parallel to each other at the intersection. When a commuter train stops at the tracks, the gate goes down and it is impossible to see another train coming on the set of parallel tracks. This isn't the first time someone has been killed at this railroad stop. Several years ago, a man was waiting at the intersection while the gate was down and the train was fully stopped. He decided to walk around the front of the stopped train, forgetting that there was another set of tracks on the other side. Unfortunately, another commuter train was traveling down those tracks and killed the man instantly. After this tragic event the railroad company plastered signs all over the intersection warning people not to go around the train because of the parallel set of tracks. The story of the twenty-seven-year old shared by my vice principal was similar except for one thing: the young man was wearing headphones. I don't believe the headphones prevented him from hearing the other train because even the parked train is quite loud, which would make it impossible for the average person to hear the whistle of the other train. I believe this young man was distracted by his headphones, so he failed to notice the great big warning signs that are plastered all over the place at this train stop.

Many children in our schools, especially in high schools, have headphones attached to their ears as they walk the halls and eat their lunch. They are in their own little world and often oblivious to what's going on around them. Although they are safe from speeding trains, they are not protected from losing important social skills or from failing to notice all of the wonderful things happening in the world around them.

A lot of parents I work with allow their children to listen to music while doing their homework because they are told by their children that it helps them to focus better. Although more research needs to be done, I don't think playing loud music helps a child solve difficult math equations or write effective English essays because it distracts the brain. If you disagree, try for yourself. The next time you are reading a novel, try listening to your favorite music at the same time. You will find this to be very difficult. I read my Kindle all the time while I am exercising on the elliptical machine at my gym and whenever a song that I know plays over the speakers I find it impossible to retain the pages I've just read. I think the real issue for kids is that they have become so used to wearing headphones all the time that they feel uncomfortable when they are not—much like the discomfort you would feel if you were to go to the supermarket barefoot. In chapter 4 I will go into detail about multitasking so that you can decide for yourself, but for now let's move on to chapter 3 so that we can get an inside look into how technology may be affecting your child's self-esteem.

CHAPTER 3

Social Media and the Development of Self-Esteem

In the first chapter we covered neuroplasticity, the brain's ability to adapt to its environment by re-wiring its circuitry, and how this may be linked to mental and emotional health issues. In this chapter we'll go over the actual content that children are exposed to through social media and how this can impact them emotionally. The content I'm referring to is not the typical online stuff we hear about like violence, pornography, and bullying; it's the innocuous, innocent stuff like selfies and tweets shared on sites like Snapchat and Twitter. These types of posts might seem harmless when compared to violent or sexual posts, but there is more than meets the eye. Let me explain.

As posts, pictures, and texts continue their endless flow between our children and others, they can pose unforeseen problems. Take, for example, the minor jokes and digs being passed around by kids. They eventually add up to something bigger because they are not one-time events; they can occur all day long, every day. And we already know that the average child is spending countless hours per day staring at the screen that is transmitting all of this. Eventually their brains and emotions absorb all of this, making it seem real. Those minor insults and slights are no longer received by the brain as just "jokes" because the minds of young people are particularly impressionable. Therefore it is important that we expose our children to genuine, face-to-face interactions with us, and their peers, and keep them away from superficial interactions as best we can. This is critical in order for our children to develop strong, resilient minds.

Even the "happy" posts that our children's friends send about their vacations, sports performances, and social gatherings are superficial and can negatively impact them. Our children are on the receiving end of hundreds, even thousands, of narcissistic photographs from their peers, which can cause them to start questioning the quality of their own life when compared to everyone else's. Their brains become overloaded and can cause them to feel insecure because eventually the brain will process all of those photos and posts like this: *Everyone else's life is so much better than mine. I am such a loser! What is wrong with me?*

In a recent CNN documentary entitled *Being 13: Inside the Secret World of Teens,* one-third of the two hundred eighth graders who were polled spent a large portion of their social media time studying their friends' and peers' social media sites to figure out where they stood in the social pecking order. They looked to see who is in and who is out, whose popularity is growing and whose is slipping.[17]

A normal part of the adolescent stage of development is figuring out where one stands in the world, where one fits in. Hours and hours a day of viewing everyone else's great life on Instagram and Snapchat can complicate this natural stage of development. Eventually our children will want to feel relevant too, and before long they will jump on board and start taking attention-seeking selfies and self-glorifying photos as a way of saying, "Hey, everyone, look at me; I have a life too." Unfortunately this plan never works because feeling good about one's self and feeling accepted does not come from outside sources; it comes from within. I'll talk more about that later.

Feeling excluded is a reality many children face if they spend too much time using social media. Take, for example, a child who comes across a post about an after-school pool party that she wasn't invited to. If that child has insecurity issues, this can feel like a real punch to the gut for her, often leading to an emotional reaction that doesn't fit the crime. I've received many phone calls from parents venting to me about situations just like this, telling me that their child had been bullied by being left out. Usually there is a rational explanation for these types of situations, but they are often overlooked because the emotional reaction to feeling rejected overshadows any explanation. Additionally, I've had dozens, maybe hundreds, of students over the last couple of years who have come my office, crying uncontrollably, after they discovered that they had been excluded from something. Obviously this is not a healthy way of dealing with rejection, but there's a reason behind this extreme reaction from today's kids.

When I was a kid in the 1980s, the biggest worry my friends and I had was getting picked last at Saturday pick-up basketball games. We didn't know the moment-to-moment details of the lives of every kid in the neighborhood, and we didn't care to. We went to school, played outside, and just enjoyed being kids. There was no front-row ticket to everyone else's "better-than-yours" vacation at the beach or their phenomenal performance at Saturday's soccer game. And parents had no outlet for showcasing their "special" child's straight As and wonderful life experiences. Life was simple. The day-to-day, moment-to-moment details of our peers' lives were out of sight and therefore out of mind, so we didn't spend our time worrying how we measured up to others. Sure we got a little jealous if a kid from class homered in the championship game, but the envy was short-lived. It was normal; it was part of being a kid and it is what helped us learn, grow, and work harder. My experiences as a child didn't have a social media half-life the way children's experiences do now. A social media post that makes a child jealous or hurts her feelings is there forever for her to review over and over again, leaving an imprint on her mind.

Adolescent life is a lot different now than it was in the 1980s. All of this exposure to everyone else's "perfect" life can cause confusion for kids, making them feel insecure about their own lives rather than gratitude for the things they have. The media, schools, and parents can further complicate this by pushing fairness and a victimization mentality rather than encouraging self-confidence and grit. We have created a trophy generation. Instead of insulating our kids from the superficial world of social media, we create rules to protect their self-esteem, and it isn't working.

My son is at the age where a lot of kids in his grade are celebrating their bar or bat mitzvahs. Some of them are his friends and some are not. A common custom at these celebrations is to give all of the kids in attendance a custom sweatshirt that represents the boy or girl being celebrated. Traditionally, the kids who attend the event would wear the sweatshirt to school the following Monday as a way of keeping the celebration alive. My son's school sends emails asking that the students not wear the sweatshirts to school because it might hurt the feelings of those students who were not invited. I don't believe this is a productive message to send because it tells the students who weren't invited that they are victims. Kids who are confident might get a little insulted for not being invited, which is normal, but because they are confident they get over it swiftly. I understand that my son's school is trying to be proactive as a way of protecting the self-esteem of those kids who weren't invited, but I believe it actually harms their self-esteem. Children need to experience rejection at times in order to develop a sense of "self" by overcoming adversity and learning from it.

A couple of years ago I coached my son's little league baseball team and often drove another kid, whom I'll call James, to practice. James, who was a fifth grader at the time, already owned a smartphone and would constantly use it in the back seat of my car every time I drove him to practice. One day I asked him what he was doing on his phone all the time, and he responded, "I'm posting pictures on my Instagram account." When I asked him why he was doing this he responded, "I don't know." But I knew. James wasn't an aspiring photographer attempting to share his artistic ability with others; James was seeking approval from others. He wanted to be noticed. He wanted to feel important. His young, vulnerable sense of self-esteem was being flattered by artificial "likes," and he was setting himself up for some insecurity issues. Let me explain why.

The word "self" is the crucial part of the term self-esteem; it is not "others"-esteem. But that is what is happening with kids these days. They often think that feeling good about themselves has something to do with how others perceive them. So instead of getting to know their true "self"—the person that they are—they compete with other kids to see who has the most "likes." They actually believe that the number of likes they have is a reflection of who they are and a barometer of their self-worth. A recent study in the *Journal of Experiential Psychology* found that having a sense of purpose limits how reactive people are to positive feedback on social media. Researchers defined a sense of purpose as ongoing motivation that is self-directed, oriented toward the future, and beneficial to others. In the study, two groups were examined, those with a high sense of purpose and those lacking a sense of purpose. All participants were asked to post a recent photo on social media and rate how they felt after getting a lot of likes or only a few likes. The participants with a high sense of purpose were unaffected whether they received a lot of likes or few likes. The participants who did not have a high sense of purpose reported feeling a greater sense of self-esteem after receiving a lot of likes and a poorer sense of self-esteem when receiving few likes. Ultimately the study found that having a high sense of purpose keeps you emotionally steady, which is important for both academic and career success.[18]

I'll conclude this section with one more story. My son, now in seventh grade, was invited to a Super Bowl party earlier this year. He has a great group of buddies who get together frequently. When I picked him up after the party was over, he didn't have the sparkle in his eyes that he normally has after he spends time with friends. When I asked him how the party was, he said, "It was ok." As I pried a little more he told me that he didn't have that much fun because the six other boys he was with were on their smartphones the entire time the game was on. He was looking forward to cheering with his friends but couldn't because he was the only one paying attention to the game. He felt alone. I often wrestle with what I should do as a parent. Sometimes I wonder if I should just get him a smartphone because I fear he might become insecure since he is the last one standing—the only kid without a phone. But I refuse to give in. I refuse to raise my son to follow the crowd. So far he is more than fine; his self-esteem is firmly intact. He has never complained about not having a phone and has never once asked for one.

FOMO – FEAR OF MISSING OUT

If this is the first time you're hearing the term FOMO, it is an acronym for Fear Of Missing Out. FOMO is a serious issue for pre-teens and teens because, as they become more enveloped in their digital interactions, the fear of missing something can cause legitimate anxiety. They become afraid to step away from a texting group chat, for example, which can go on forever, because they fear they will become isolated or irrelevant. They crave the constant communication and attention they receive, but the problem is that it isn't face-to-face, which is the only form of human interaction that can foster confidence, emotional regulation, and empathy. I will explain this in more depth in chapter 7. Furthermore, the text chats and social media posts often become argumentative and sometimes downright abusive, which further damages kids' self-esteem. The hurtful comments feel quite real to kids even though in most cases their peers who post them would never say such things in person.

Those kids who are immersed in the social-media world often stay up until the wee hours of the morning because they can't get themselves to let go of the craving to be part of something. This causes sleep deprivation, academic issues, and sometimes anxiety and depression. It is a cycle that becomes very difficult to break. Do you have a child that is too connected to his or her social media life? See for yourself below.

WARNING SIGNS

Here are some warning signs that your child is spending too much time using any form of electronic media, including television, video games, handheld devices, and computers/tablets.

- Loses track of time when using electronic devices
- Becomes agitated when interrupted

- Prefers to spend time using electronics rather than being with friends or family in person

- Does not follow time limits

- Forms relationships with people online

- Loss of interest in other activities

- Seems restless when not using a device and preoccupied with getting back on

- Avoids homework and chores because of spending too much time with electronics

- Sneaks on a device when no one is around and lies about it

If your child exhibits any of these signs, you will need to step in. The best way to address any of these issues is to sit down with your child and express your concerns. Next, set strict guidelines for your child to follow and make it clear that if he or she violates them that there will be consequences. Guidelines might include no electronics in the bedroom, no video games during the week, no smartphones in the car or during dinner, and mandatory unplugging times. Should your child violate any of the guidelines you must hold him accountable and follow the consequences you prescribed. Consequences might include removing the television from the bedroom, taking away the cellphone for a week, or unplugging the video game console for a period of time. Consistency is the key. I will discuss how to help your children (and yourself!) cut down on electronic media consumption in greater detail in Part Three of this book.

LEGAL CONSEQUENCES

Stephen was a seventeen-year-old high school junior when I started seeing him for counseling. Although his parents were married, they didn't see eye-to-eye and had very inconsistent parenting styles, which led to a lot of problems for Stephen. They were referred to me because Stephen continually got into trouble with his peers due to the inappropriate comments he posted on social media. Because Stephen's self-esteem was low, he struggled to form friendships and social media became his outlet. It was the perfect platform for him to express whatever he wanted to, which was often attention-seeking messages and photos, to which he received a tremendous amount of negative feedback from peers. But attention is attention and for a lot of teenagers it doesn't matter if the attention is positive or negative; they are still being noticed, making them feel relevant instead of invisible.

After attending one of my lectures, Stephen's parents finally came to the realization that all of the time Stephen was spending on his computer and phone were greatly affecting him. He lied to them all the time about what he was doing in his online world. He would sneak the devices and use them when he was not permitted to. I myself noticed that when he came to my office, Stephen would be wearing a big pair of Beats headphones, totally disengaged from his parents even though he was sitting right next to them in the waiting room. All of the deception that came from his social media addiction was having an enormous impact on his relationship with his parents.

After his parents informed me that they had found inappropriate content on Stephen's phone directed toward a younger girl, I urged the parents to take away his devices. I explained to them that doing so would make things a lot worse at first because he would undoubtedly become agitated, make threats, and try to manipulate them, which is exactly what he did. The day after our appointment Stephen's father called to tell me that Stephen had gone ballistic after they took away his devices. Words came out of his mouth that no parent could ever imagine, and he refused to go to school if his devices were not returned to him. He even threatened to harm himself. After a few days his parents couldn't take it any longer and gave him his devices back.

At our next session I urged Stephen to be very careful with any content he transmitted. Since he had just turned eighteen a couple of days before, I explained to him that he could get into a lot of trouble, particularly if he distributed any inappropriate content to a minor, because he was now a legal adult. He denied doing any of this.

Five days later, I learned from Stephen's parents that the police had arrived at their house with a search warrant to confiscate Stephen's laptop. A young girl had reported him to the police for making sexually explicit comments and more. Stephen was arrested and placed in jail. It was Stephen's poor self-esteem that led him to his online obsession. In his online world, he was relevant; people knew who he was, but it worked against him. Although Stephen's story is an extreme example of social-media use gone bad, examples like this are very real, as one bad decision can affect you for the rest of your life.

Although stories like Stephen's are downright awful, it can be worse. Frightening new data about a dramatic rise in suicide rates among adolescents was recently published by the Centers for Disease Control and Prevention. In 1999 the death rate from traffic accidents for children ages ten to fourteen was quadruple the rate for suicide. Over the last fifteen years, the suicide rate for children in this age group has caught up to their death rate from traffic accidents. While the death rate from traffic accidents has been cut in half since 1999, the suicide rate has nearly doubled since 2007, leading to the crossover point. The CDC points to evidence that young adolescents are suffering from a range of health problems because of the country's rapidly changing culture. The pervasiveness of social media allows the entire school to now witness someone's shame instead of a small group of girls on the school bus. And as children continue to have more access to new and different social media networks, the pressures continue when the child comes home from school. Although far more boys kill themselves than girls do, the CDC's data found that the increase for girls has tripled while the rise for boys has increased by a third.[19] According to Rachel Simmons, the author of *Odd Girl Out: The Hidden Culture of Aggression in Girls*, "Social media is girl town."[20] Because girls statistically dominate visual platforms like Instagram and Facebook, Simmons states that they receive instant validation from peers and take things that were once private and make them public. For girls who are vulnerable, quantifying one's popularity through social media can be very destabilizing.

Folks, we have got to get a handle on this issue. We have to remember that we the parents are the ones that call the shots. If your child is the only one without a smartphone and all of the social media outlets that it provides constant access to, good. She will be just fine. In fact she will be better than fine: she will develop a solid sense of self. If your child is obsessed with his smartphone and social media interactions, it is not too late to intervene. It won't be easy, but it is doable. In the final chapters I will show you how.

CHAPTER 4

The Multitasking Brains of Kids

Just about every time I lecture to parent groups, the following question comes up: "Why does my child get four or five hours of homework a night?" My answer? He doesn't! I explain to the audience that although it might take your child that long to complete his homework, he probably only has one or two hours of homework, but it takes him much longer to complete because he is multitasking while doing his homework. That's right—kids are posting, texting, listening to music, and watching YouTube while they are doing homework, and for some crazy reason we turn a blind eye to this. There's a lot of science that proves multitasking affects not only schoolwork, but also kids' brains.

The late Clifford Nass, a professor at Stanford University, conducted some impressive research on multitasking. Nass defined multitasking as the use of unrelated media content. In other words, if a teenager listens to music while switching back and forth between Facebook, text messages, and emails, that would be considered multitasking between different, unrelated media content. Chronic task switching affects the front area of the brain that is responsible for executive functioning. This is the area of the brain that helps us organize our working memory, switch from one task to another smoothly, and focus on relevant information.[21]

Nass conducted experiments with his students that demonstrated how the frontal area of the brain functions and how it is affected by multitasking. One of Nass's experiments was simple. His students were asked to look at slides that consisted of two red rectangles and some blue rectangles; they were instructed to focus only on the red rectangles and determine how many times they had moved with each ensuing slide. Two groups of students participated: high multitaskers and low multitaskers. The high multitaskers all believed that multitasking helped them perform better academically, but the experiment proved them wrong. High multitaskers struggled immensely with this simple experiment when more blue rectangles were added from slide to slide. Their brains could not help but get distracted by the blue rectangles, and the more that were added the worse they did. Low multitaskers were unaffected by the blue rectangles no matter how many were added; they were able to focus on the red rectangles as instructed and accurately determine how many times the red rectangles had rotated.

Nass decided to further prove his theory with another experiment that included the use of an fMRI (functional magnetic resonance imaging) device. In the experiment both groups were given a simple task-switching exercise while connected to the fMRI device, and the results were impressive. High multitaskers used twenty times more of their brain while engaging in the experiment than low multitaskers. But there was an unforeseen outcome: they were using the wrong part of the brain, the part known as the visual cortex. Low multitaskers needed only a small amount of brainpower to complete the task, and it was the area of the brain they were supposed to be using, the pre-frontal cortex. In other words, the high multitasking students were actually worse at multitasking than the low multitasking students.

Imagine how hard it must be for high multitasking students to sit down and focus on completing homework efficiently and effectively when their brains don't work that way. They struggle immensely. I can tell you that it isn't teachers giving too much homework that is causing so many kids to "have too much homework." Here is an example. Nass used another experiment, a classic experiment created by Daniel J. Simons, called The Monkey Business Illusion. Before you continue to read, navigate to this link and follow the instructions: http://bit.ly/M9rlws.

How did you do? Did you guess the correct number of passes? If not, you are probably a high multitasker. If you succeeded, then you are likely a low multitasker. In case you did not get a chance to try the experiment, here's how it works:

There are six young ladies standing in a line. Three of them are wearing white tee shirts and one of them is holding a basketball. The other three are wearing black tee shirts and one is holding a basketball. In the experiment you are asked to count how many times the girls in white pass the basketball back and forth to each other. What makes the task challenging is that the girls wearing black are also passing the ball amongst each other, which can be distracting. As all six are passing the ball to their respective teammates, they are also walking between one another, making it even more confusing. High multitaskers fail miserably at counting the correct number of passes between the girls wearing white tee shirts because their brains can't help but be distracted by the girls in black along with other distractions happening in the video. Low multitaskers have no problem counting the correct number of passes between the girls wearing white.

Nass's experiment highlighted another difference between the brains of high and low multitaskers. In the video, while the basketball is passed around among both the white and black groups, there are three other things occurring. First, a person wearing a black gorilla suit walks right through the group of young ladies. Next, one of the young ladies from the black tee shirt group leaves the stage. Lastly, the color of the curtain in the background changes color. Watch the video again and see for yourself. High multitaskers were good at noticing the gorilla and the other anomalies, but they were bad at correctly counting the number of passes between the white players. Low multitaskers were good at counting the passes correctly but did not notice the gorilla, the girl in black leaving the stage, or the curtain changing colors. Ultimately, high multitaskers were bad at managing memory. If you look at the brain as a file cabinet that neatly stores necessary information, the brains of high multitaskers are a mess. The executive functioning area of the brain is compromised.

Researchers have also conducted studies with drivers. They looked at MRIs of drivers to see how much brain attention went towards driving. When another bit of information was layered in, like listening to music, the amount of brain bandwidth going towards driving dropped by 37 percent.[22] So all of a sudden, the drivers aren't really multitasking, they're now paying less attention to driving. Have you ever tried watching a movie while simultaneously scanning through Facebook? It's almost impossible to pay attention to the movie.

A guidance counselor at my school invited me to a meeting recently with a concerned mom. The mom was worried about her fourteen-year-old daughter's academic struggles. The girl's teachers also attended the meeting. The mom explained that although her daughter was a smart girl, she often became overwhelmed and would shut down. The mom also explained that a simple fifteen-minute homework assignment took her daughter two hours to complete, and the girl agreed that she wasn't exaggerating.

The student's math teacher, who spoke first, stated that the girl was constantly distracted in class by her laptop. The teacher had to continuously tell her to close it. (In my school district, each student is provided a personal laptop). The next teacher stated that all was fine in her class. The final three teachers also claimed that the laptop was a major distraction for the girl. After the teachers gave their accounts, I chimed in and asked the mom if her daughter was distracted by her smartphone or laptop while doing homework. The mom stated that she was.

This brief meeting told me a lot. Here we had a fourteen-year-old girl whose brain was all over the place. She had over twenty missing homework assignments because she forgot about them. It took her forever to complete simple assignments that should have taken minutes. This girl's brain file cabinet, the pre-frontal cortex, was a mess. The constant task switching was dividing this girl's attention across many different types of stimuli, reducing her ability to focus on one specific task, schoolwork. Rather than processing material and storing it in her long-term memory bank, this girl was sending the information from all of these different sources, including schoolwork, to the wrong part of the brain where it could not be stored long-term and retrieved later.

Talk to any veteran high school or college English teacher and they will tell you that many students struggle to produce essays that are well organized and logically argued. Essays are often fragmented, disorganized messes, which makes sense when you imagine writing a three-page paper while constantly task switching between writing and checking social media content. This continual switching interrupts the flow of writing and leads to papers that miss the fundamental essentials of proper writing: an introductory statement, a body, and a conclusion.

Multitasking also leads to a type of "fragmented" thinking. Because tweets, posts, texts, and likes are all done in short, quick bursts, over time the brain becomes accustomed to short bursts of communication, causing it to think in fragmented ways. According to Dr. Gary Small, "It's a basic principle that the brain is very sensitive to any kind of stimulation, and from moment to moment, there is a very complex cascade of neurochemical electrical consequences to every form of stimulation. If you have repeated stimuli, your neural circuits will be excited. But if you neglect other stimuli, other neural circuits will be weakened."[23] Dr. Elias Aboujaoude, director of Stanford University's Impulse Control Disorders Clinic, agrees. According to Aboujaoude, "The more we become used to just sound bites and tweets, the less patient we will be with more complex, more meaningful information. And I do think we might lose the ability to analyze things with any depth and nuance. Like any skill, if you don't use it, you lose it."[24]

Research conducted by The University of London dramatizes just how damaging multitasking can be. One study found that participants who multitasked during cognitive tasks experienced IQ score declines that were similar to what researchers would expect to see if the study subjects had smoked marijuana or stayed up all night. IQ drops of 15 points for multitasking adults lowered their scores to the average range of an eight-year-old child. As Dr. Travis Bradberry, best-selling author of *Emotional Intelligence 2.0,* commented about this research, "[The] next time you're writing your boss an email during a meeting, remember that your cognitive capacity is being diminished to the point that you might as well let an eight-year-old write it for you."[25]

Jeff Guo has used similar research to argue that students shouldn't use laptops to take notes. Economists from West Point conducted a large experiment that demonstrated how classroom computing affects learning. They randomly banned computers from some sections of a popular economics course this past year at the military academy. One third of the cadets were allowed to use laptops or tablets for note-taking during lectures, one third could use them only to look at class material, and one third were prohibited from using any technology. Not surprising, the students who were allowed to use the laptops or tablets did worse on the final exam. Interestingly, the smartest students seemed to be harmed the most. Among the students who had high ACT scores, those who were allowed to use their laptops or tablets performed significantly worse than their peers in the no-technology section. What's strange about these results is that one would expect the smartest students who were in the laptop-friendly section to use these machines more prudently. Instead, they were the biggest victims of technology because they overestimated their ability to multitask. Or, according to Guo, "the top students might have had the most to gain by paying attention in class."[26]

Another way to look at the West Point results is by using the average score on the math section of the SAT from last year. That score was 511 out of 800. According to Guo, "The difference between exam grades in the laptop-friendly sections and exam grades in the no-laptop sections is the equivalent to the difference between scoring a 511 and scoring a 491 on the SAT's math section. (That's roughly the same boost a high school student might expect from hiring an SAT tutor.)" This is more evidence that multitasking doesn't work. Guo warns, "Beware of people who take laptops into meetings—even to take notes, because they're probably not listening to you." So multitasking is bad not only for kids but for adults too.

A study published in *Psychological Science* supports this. The study sought to test how note-taking by hand or by computer affects learning. The researchers selected university students and asked them to take notes from a series of TED talks they were shown. The students who used a laptop to take notes did substantially poorer answering conceptual-application questions when compared to students who took notes by hand. The evidence suggested that taking notes by hand produced superior external storage as well as superior encoding functions when compared to taking notes with a laptop.[27] In other words, our brains are much better at learning and retaining information when we take notes by hand.

Finally, Common Sense Media's 2014 white paper—which reviews existing studies on media use, technology, and addiction—concludes that there is cause for concern with regard to too much media use because of the potentially damaging consequences. The paper finds that multitasking, which is common for kids while doing homework and while socializing, affects their learning, their schoolwork, and their memory. In addition, too much media use can undermine empathy and reduce face-to-face conversation. Ellen Wartella, a leading scholar of the role of media in children's development, agrees that multitasking affects attention, social skills and interpersonal skills and that we must continue to research the impact of media on our kids..[28]

PART TWO

Technology's Effect on Social, Emotional, and Family Growth

CHAPTER 5

Gamer Kids: The Great Human Disconnect

Alex was a sixteen-year-old high school junior who hadn't been to school in six weeks. After the school psychologist, assistant principal, and I met with his father it became obvious what the problem was—video games. Alex spent so much time playing video games he had become addicted. According to his father, Alex played for a minimum of twelve hours per day, seven days a week. Alex gained a lot of weight and became depressed, which contributed to his anxiety and subsequent school avoidance. The video games that were once just a fun way to spend time had become a drug for him. They became his escape from the world, and everything around him began to crumble—school, health, family, and social life. Interestingly, his father did not connect the dots until after we met with him; he did not realize that Alex's video game obsession was the source of his problems.

You may be wondering how a parent could allow their child to play twelve hours of video games per day. You'd be surprised how many parents are oblivious to the amount of time their children spend gaming. Alex's father presumed that because his son was home all the time that he was simply bored and had nothing else to do to pass the time. He didn't understand that it was the other way around. Being home with all of that free time didn't lead to his video game addiction; his video game addiction led him to be home all the time and therefore to disconnect from the world outside of his bedroom.

Recently I received a phone call from the parents of a seventeen-year-old boy who was referred to me by someone who attended one of my lectures. They wanted to schedule an appointment with me to discuss options for their video-game-addicted son. The session I had with them was troubling. Their son had not been to school in over two years and was receiving home instruction. He barely ate and had lost a tremendous amount of weight because he was unable to pull himself away from his gaming console.

The boy's video game playing had gotten so out of control when he was in middle school that by the time he reached high school he refused to go. Any time his parents attempted to take away his beloved video game console he would go berserk. He punched holes in the wall and became verbally and physically violent. His parents were scared of their son and called the police on several occasions. The saddest part was that the couple had separated and were pursuing divorce because their son's addiction had ripped into their marriage. At the time of our visit, their son was a full-blown agoraphobic; he hadn't left the house in months. I never got a chance to help the boy because his parents were unable to get him to my office.

When parents call me for help with their video game addicted children, I know they are hoping that I have some magic powers that will make the problem go away. What I've learned through my experiences is that most parents of video game addicts are afraid to take away their child's games for fear of what the child might do. You see, the reaction often resembles that of a crack addict whose crack has been taken away. One parent told me that after her son had begun failing all of his subjects, she decided it was time to unplug the Xbox. Her son—whom she and his teachers described as calm, friendly, and respectful—went bonkers. He cursed out his mom, destroyed the coffee table in the family room, and punched holes in his bedroom wall. Another mother told me that after she removed her son's games, her son took a knife out of the kitchen drawer and threatened to stab her with it. And still other parents have told me that when they've taken away their child's games, their child threatened to commit suicide. There is something gravely wrong here. Many of you reading this know exactly what I am talking about because you have experienced similar situations with your own sons or daughters.

Taiwan's video game addiction epidemic has prompted the government to create laws that hold parents accountable if their children spend too much time gaming.[29] Some Asian countries have created boot-camp style rehabilitation centers for video game addicted kids. There are stories of teenagers soiling themselves and nearly starving themselves because they were unable to detach themselves from their games, even for just a few minutes. One Asian teen was so addicted to his video games that he chopped off his own hand so that he could stop playing. Thankfully, doctors were able to reattach his hand.[30] Video game addiction causes reclusiveness and social anxiety, and many gaming addicts socialize with "friends" through headsets and have no real-life social interactions. Parents feel paralyzed, fearing that if they take away their child's games then their child will become lonely and depressed because they will have no one to associate with.

Many of the preteens and teens that I counsel are well aware of their gaming addiction and the impact it is having on their lives, yet they still cannot get themselves to stop playing. As parents, we must step in and take control of these kinds of situations no matter how difficult it is. Here are some comments taken verbatim from real teenagers that I found on www.video-game-addiction.org:

"I am 14 and I'm a freaken addict . . . my parents seem to care but never try to kick me off or even try to help. i have 2 lvl 70's one that is full t6 and other full t5. Thus I have no life. I cant even imagine what I would do if I deleted my toons. I really want to quit but I can't. I mean this [expletive deleted] game is controlling me and I cant' stop. I have almost deleted my toons but I'm afraid I'll just start up another one."

"I'm 12 and I cant stop playing. Wow i play about 8-10 hours a day mostly because all my friends are on it, and I'm bored when I don't play. I just failed socials too so what should I do?"

"WOW addiction is no joke. I started to play because cousins and friends played (who are by the way all overweight). At first all I did was play WOW (World of Warcraft) once or twice a day for lets say 2-3 hours. Then out of the blue my cousin stopped playing because he said he was addicted to WOW, so he gave me his 70 (rogue). Well after that I was on 6-10 hours a day. I ignored my friends, went from working out 4 times a week to twice. I would cuss people who asked me to get off. In the end though I realized by playing WOW I was just supporting big Business. Also, why waste money, time with friends for a game? I know people who would be a lot better off without WOW. I just want to try to get all the money I have invested into it back so I am going to sell the (rogue) ... "

"I want to quit WOW so badly. I've been playing for 2 years ... The problem is that I don't know what else to do besides play video games :(."

"I ended up ill with a deep vein thrombosis in one of my legs caused, according to the Doctors by me sitting on my backside doing instances all night and all day."[31]

According to the NPD Group, a market research company, there are thirty-four million hardcore gamers who spend an average of twenty-two hours a week in front of the screen. China and the United States claim 50 percent of the world's gaming revenues, and by 2018 the video gaming market is expected to hit $113.3 billion.[32] The *Diagnostic and Statistical Manuel (DSM-5)*, which offers the common language and standard criteria for the classification of mental disorders, describes "internet gaming disorder" as a "condition for further study." In other words, it is on the radar of the American Psychological Association, the organization that publishes the DSM. Much like any addiction, when gaming begins to interfere with important life areas such as relationships, health, or school we know it has become a serious problem. Furthermore, gaming can pose self-esteem and relationship issues because it can allow players to act differently than they would normally act in real life. A shy kid can become unreserved, and a timid kid can become aggressive while gaming, for example.

Many socially awkward kids that I have counseled over the years discover the virtual world where they can be more expressive, lead armies to victory, and be leaders of a specific game. Playing these video games creates a feeling of real accomplishment even though there is nothing real about it. In fact, the same neurons in the brain that would fire from actually hitting the game-ending homerun in real life will fire from maneuvering a game controller. Many parents of gaming addicts tell me that their child has no real friends because no one calls, no one comes over the house, and no one invites their child anywhere. The idea of taking away their games is a tough one because parents feel that by doing so they are taking away the only "friends" their child has and the only thing their child is good at.

Sadly, a child who spends all of his time socializing through a headset and screen, and no time engaged in face-to-face interaction, will not develop the necessary communication skills that are required to succeed in the real world. Just the thought of face-to-face interaction for kids like these can cause serious distress. It goes back to the science of neuroplasticity—if you don't use it you lose it. Furthermore, if virtual success from being good at a specific video game is the only feeling of success your child has, you can bet that your child's self-esteem will continue to suffer as he or she will have very few real life successes.

PHYSICAL REALITIES

A new study published in the journal *Plos One* outlines researchers' discovery that sleep deprivation caused by video game addiction may increase obesity and lead to cardio-metabolic deficits. In the study, researchers collected data from ninety-four adolescents between the ages of twelve and seventeen. They used surveys, Fitbit sleep monitors, physical exams, and blood tests. After analyzing all of the data, the researchers found that video game addiction was negatively associated with sleep duration, which was related to an elevation in blood pressure, LDL cholesterol, triglycerides, and high insulin resistance. Ultimately, video game addiction can lead to future obesity, heart disease, and type II diabetes.[33]

If you are concerned about your child's video game use, here are some things to look out for.

- Outside of school, the majority of hours are spent on the computer or playing video games

- Drop in grades in school

- Lack of focus in school

- Sleeping in school

- Lying about video game/computer use

- Choosing to socialize with video game friends rather than with real friends

- Dropping out of sports and extracurricular activities

- Throws tantrums when told to turn off gaming

- Being irritable when not playing games

If you are the parent of a child who spends too much time playing video games, and you are afraid that unplugging these games is going make matters worse, it is a risk you are going to have to take. Yes, your child may throw a tantrum and make your life miserable, but this will not last forever. It is something you are going to have to deal with and you will be thankful later on.

CHAPTER 6

Parenting from a Distance

Whenever I go to a restaurant with my family I want to jump out of my seat with a bullhorn and shout, "WOULD EVERYONE PLEASE GET YOUR HEADS OUT OF YOUR ASSES!" That's because every time I go out to eat the majority of people, both children and adults, are staring at a tablet or smartphone and not talking to one other. It drives me crazy. When did it become ok to replace our family members with a screen?

At a recent dinner out with my family, the man sitting at the table to my right was attempting to have a conversation with his wife while her eyes moved back and forth between him and the text chat she was having. The man's wife probably didn't hear a word he said, and the man didn't even realize it. To my left was a table of four women and a young girl. Two of the women continuously glanced towards their laps where their smartphones were concealed as they pretended to be interested in the conversation occurring with their friends at the table. The young girl that was with them had a pair of ear buds in her ears and a tablet in front of her the entire time. She seemed oblivious to her surroundings because she was hypnotized by the game she was playing. When the waitress placed her entrée in front of her it took the girl a couple of minutes to realize it had arrived. Finally, there was a couple with two young children sitting directly across from us. Both children were quietly fixated on tablets as the couple enjoyed their "alone" time together without any interruptions from their kids.

My family and I love dining out for two reasons: we love to eat, and we love to be together. Being together means talking, laughing, and communicating with one another, not avoiding each other. Sadly, I can't remember the last time I was at a restaurant where the majority of the patrons weren't distracted by their devices. See for yourself the next time you dine out. Really take note of the lack of communication and interaction, particularly between parents and their children. Most parents do not realize that this is a problem because they are not properly educated, which is why I give my lectures. Historically, the dinner table has been the ideal place to communicate with our children and get to know what is going on in their lives, but that has changed. According to Norman Herr of California State University at Northridge, the average parent spends just three-and-a-half minutes per week in meaningful conversation with their children.[34] Yes, per *week*! And it doesn't help that some chain restaurants now have tablets built right into the table in front of each seat. Talk about taking away the most important part of dinner—spending time and communicating with the people we love.

We all know that a quick way to calm down a crying or unruly child is to park them in front of a tablet or television screen. Occasionally this is fine, but have we gone too far? The next time you're driving, take a look inside the cars around you, particularly if traffic is moving slowly. You will notice the passengers, and sometimes the driver, scrolling through their phones. If there are young children in the back seat you will see that they are either fixated on the TV screen, which is built into the back headrest, or their iPad. There is nothing wrong with allowing our children some screen time during long drives, but that's not the issue here. It is happening during every ride, even the five-minute rides to school or soccer practice.

The dinner table and car rides are two of the most important places in the world for parents because they present the perfect opportunities to talk to our children about their day, see what is on their minds, and form connections with them. Yet we are allowing screens to take this away from us. I see it every morning when I am pulling into the high school parking lot. There is always a lot of traffic as there are 1,300 students and staff all converging at the same time.

When I look in my rearview mirror I see the same image all the time—a stressed-out parent driving the car and their teenage child in the front seat wearing a set of headphones and peering into their phone. There's no communication, no connection.

The American Academy of Pediatrics recommends avoiding screens prior to eighteen months old and keeping it to only an hour up to age five.[35] Yet countless babies, toddlers, and teens stare into these machines for multiple hours a day, seven days a week.

COACHING DILEMMA

My favorite pastime is baseball. As a child I couldn't get enough of it, and I was talented. I played for one of the top high school baseball programs in the country and went on to play in college. After my son was born in 2003, he had a bat in his hand before he knew how to drink from a bottle. Today, I am one of the coaches for his travel baseball team. The team and the families are very close, as the boys have been playing together for five years. When we travel to play in tournaments we often stay overnight at hotels and go out together for meals. The boys usually sit together at one table and the adults at another. The boys have always been quite loud and goofy at their table, which is to be expected. Last year, when the boys were in sixth grade, all of them, except for my son, got their first smartphones. The once loud dinner table of twelve boys had suddenly gone quiet as each of them became mesmerized by the screens in front of them and disengaged from one another.

During last year's summer season I couldn't take it anymore. I could not stand to watch all of these wonderful boys sitting at a table together and opting to play videogames on their phones instead of talking to each other about school, baseball, and life. I didn't think it was my place to say anything to the boys at first because they were not my children, but then it hit me—I am their coach. I can tell them what they can or can't do when we are together as a team whether it's on the field or in a restaurant. So I stood up one night at the table where I was sitting with the other parents and in my coach's voice I told all of my players to hand their phones over to their parents right then and start talking to each other again. Much to my surprise, the parents all thanked me for doing this. Not one of them was upset with me. Now, whenever we go out to eat as a team or family there are no electronic devices allowed at the table. And guess what? The boys love it. They laugh, they goof around, they talk, they do what boys are supposed to do.

The message here is very simple. Our children need to communicate with other children, face-to-face, and they need to do it a lot because it is critical to their social and emotional development. We can no longer just turn a blind eye and ignore this important issue. We can no longer just allow our children to be disengaged from their peers and from us and be pacified by a screen. I'm glad I stood up at that restaurant that night and took care of this situation with my team because it sent a powerful message not only to the boys, but also to the parents. So don't be afraid to speak out when you are with your friends and their children. Your friends will thank you for it, and you will set a good example for your children to always stand up for your beliefs.

FAMILY TIME

Over the last few years I've had an incredible number of referrals to my private practice for teenagers who are struggling with everyday life. I like to meet with the parents first so that I can get a clear picture of the problems their child is experiencing. The problem usually has something to do with anxiety, depression, or behavior, and the cause is usually tied to social media or video games. The stories I hear are unbelievable, like the sixteen-year-old who played a specific video game forty hours a week or the boy who developed a fake identity online and came to believe his own lies. The parents feel helpless and ask me what they can do to help their son or daughter. The answer that I give them is very simple: *talk to them*.

The atmosphere in today's typical American household is much different than in previous generations. Not many adults are sitting on their porches during the week, socializing with the neighbors. Few kids are running around the neighborhood playing manhunt, dreading the sound of mom's voice at 6:00 p.m. when she calls them in for dinner. Instead, families are cooped up inside their homes, screens in hands, isolated from each other. The American family no longer looks like a family. If I were to put hidden cameras in some homes to get a glimpse at the new American family, it would look something like this: mom, dad, and the kids are all disconnected from each other and connected to a computer screen, tablet, smartphone, or video game console. Dad might be watching the ball game, mom might be on the computer, and the kids are texting, playing video games, or spending hours of time on YouTube and Snapchat. Although these families live under the same roof, they barely know each other.

Think I'm exaggerating? Find me a teenager who is not locked away in his or her bedroom each night, completely disassociated from the rest of the family. Somewhere along the way this has become common, but just because it is common does not mean that it is normal. Parenting 101 says that a child, no matter what age, should not have any electronics whatsoever in his or her bedroom. Yet we ignore this advice because we just don't understand the dangers. More and more children, particularly teens, are becoming reclusive and barely speak to their parents. They become addicted to their devices and the attention they are getting from those on the other end. For many of us, our families are falling apart right in front of our eyes and we don't even realize it is happening. Perhaps we too are busy attending to our own digital world and forget that our children need our attention. Parents, if you take just one thing from everything you've read so far, it should be this: *get your kids out of the bedroom* and into the family room. There's a reason why we have "family" rooms and bedrooms. One is for spending time with family and the other is for sleeping. And please limit your own media use when you are at home.

A recent survey conducted by Common Sense Media found that teens feel addicted to their phones, causing tension at home. The Common Sense poll surveyed 1,240 parents and kids from the same households and found that 50 percent of the teens "feel addicted" to mobile devices, and 59 percent of their parents agreed that their kids are addicted. Furthermore, more than one-third of the families surveyed were concerned about the effects that mobile device use was having on their daily lives whether it was driving, schoolwork, or the dinner table. As James Steyer, founder and CEO of Common Sense Media, puts it, "Mobile devices are fundamentally changing how families go about their day-to-day lives."[36]

The key findings from the Common Sense survey are as follows:

- *Addiction:* One out of every two teens feels addicted to his or her device, and the majority of parents (59 percent) feel that their kids are addicted.

- *Frequency:* 72 percent of teens and 48 percent of parents feel the need to immediately respond to texts, social media messages and other notifications. 69 percent of parents and 78 percent of teens check their devices at least hourly.

- *Distraction:* 77 percent of parents feel their children get distracted by their devices and don't pay attention when they are together at least a few times per week.

- *Conflict:* One-third of parents and teens say they argue with each other on a daily basis about device use.

- *Risky behavior:* 56 percent of parents admit they check their mobile devices while driving; 51 percent of teens witness this.

Remember the teenage boy I mentioned earlier who had his phone taken away by his parents and left the suicide note? After it came out that the boy spent all of his time in his bedroom, I gave the parents some simple advice. I told them to have mandatory family talk time every night. They followed my advice, the boy reluctantly started coming out of his room, and the whole family started to get to know each other. The result? The boy got better. Folks, our children need us. They need to have conversations with us, and we need to have conversations with them. Think about your own family for a minute and ask yourself the following questions:

1. Do you sit down and have meaningful conversations with your children on a daily basis?

2. Does your child spend a lot of time, alone, in his or her bedroom?

3. Do you spend a lot of time, alone, in front of a screen?

How have we gotten to this point? There are several variables. First, more parents of this generation have a hard time saying "no" to their children. We fear that saying no is going to harm the relationship we have with them. Next, all of this technology and all of these devices have made their way into our lives at such a lightning-fast pace we simply didn't see it coming. Finally, the addictive nature of all this technology and the conflicts that ensue have become so common that it almost seems normal. I can assure you it is not normal.

THE DINNER TABLE

A couple of years ago I was selected to host a television pilot for Food Network called *Can Dinner Save My Family.* The purpose of the show was to transform a family in need by requiring them to commit to having dinner together for thirty straight days. Although Food Network did not develop the pilot into a series, they did air the episode, which focused on a single mother of three who was having a hard time with her troubled fifteen-year-old son. He had recently been released from a juvenile detention center and the mother was desperate to repair her relationship with him. The family was instructed by me to prepare and eat dinner together for thirty straight days. The premise of the show was to document how families who have dinner together on a regular basis function much better. The thirty-day dinner intervention worked for this family; they became closer, argued less, and communicated better.

Studies have shown that children who regularly eat dinner with their families are less likely to engage in risky behavior, less likely to develop mental health disorders, and more likely to do better in school and be happier overall. Unfortunately, many of us are spread so thin between work and chauffeuring our children around from dance rehearsal to soccer practice that we don't have the time to sit together for dinner on a consistent basis, or at all. Those of us who do often allow the TV to be on or handheld devices to be used during the meal. The dinner table needs to be a sacred place because it gives us an opportunity to know what is going on in our children's lives. When televisions and other screens are mixed in with dinnertime, the important communication needed by both our children and ourselves is reduced. Start making it a habit to have dinner together most nights of the week and establish a rule that no electronic devices are allowed during family mealtime.

As a child, family dinner was mandatory in the Kersting household—every night. My brother and sisters and I had to be at the dinner table every night at 6:00 p.m., no matter what. Before we ate, we would all hold hands and my father would say grace, thanking the Lord above for our wonderful food and family. In today's fast-paced world it can seem impossible to have set family dinner—I get it. But I'm here to say that it's not impossible. In my household, we eat together almost every night. Although it's not at a set time like it was when I was a child, we still pull it off. Some nights I don't get home until 8:00 p.m., and although this is late, we still try to eat together because my wife and I know the importance of this ritual. During dinner, no television or electronics are allowed. We talk and we eat. I get to learn about my children's days and they get to learn about mine. But most important of all we get to know each other and connect with each other because we are disconnected from cyberspace.

CATCHING THE MOMENT

A couple of years ago I took a trip to an indoor waterpark with my parents, brother and sisters, and all of our children. My brother and

I were racing around the park with our boys, hopping from one waterslide to another. My brother had a waterproof camera with him and was preparing to use it on one of the more popular rides. Right before he was about to go down the slide with his son he had the camera ready to go. When we met at the bottom of the slide I asked him if he had "caught the moment." He responded, "I certainly did." I then said, "Joe, do you realize that by 'catching the moment' you actually missed the moment?" He looked at me, confused.

Do you miss the moment with your kids? Are you fully immersed in the present moment when you are with them or are you distracted by your smartphone or computer? If the communication flowing in your home resembles the waiting room at your dentist's office, then you are missing the moment with your children. You are missing them grow. You are growing apart from your children, and they are growing apart from you. Your home becomes nothing more than a daily gathering of strangers fixated on a bunch of machines.

Whenever I watch my favorite team on television, the New York Yankees, I love to observe the fans behind home plate. I notice that many of them aren't actually watching the game. Instead they are taking photos and selfies to show everyone how amazing their seats are and how amazing they are as a result. Additionally, if they aren't snapping pictures from their close-up seats, they are texting or using social media while the game is being played. It happens at all sporting events. Just watch an NBA basketball game and pay attention to the fans who are sitting courtside. Many of them are staring at their phones and missing the game. One YouTube clip someone showed me had me laughing out loud. A woman was attending a basketball game and a loose ball went into the crowd and smacked her right in the face because she was watching her phone, not the game. The cameraman just so happened to catch the whole ordeal perfectly. When watched in slow motion you can see the ball as it hits the woman squarely in the face. Thankfully, the woman wasn't hurt, but the footage was hysterical. The point I'm making is that we miss many moments, including game-winning shots, because we are either trying to catch the moment on camera or we are distracted.

A company called Yondr has decided to do something about this and has a simple purpose: to show people how powerful a moment can be when they aren't documenting or broadcasting it. As people enter a venue their phones are placed in Yondr cases. Once they enter the phone-free zone, the cases will lock. Attendees maintain possession of their phones but are free to enjoy the event without distraction. If at any point attendees need to use their phone, they simply step outside the phone-free zone and unlock the case. Although famous rock stars and comedians love it, the company has been renting its devices to schools, restaurants, wedding venues, and sporting events as well. Graham Dugoni, the founder of Yondr, says of his company's mission, "I view it as a social movement, and this is one piece of the puzzle. It's about helping people live in the digital age in a way that doesn't hollow out all of the meaning in your life."[37] Folks, if we put our minds to it we wouldn't need Yondr cases. All we need to do is to learn a little self control and teach this to our children.

I'm sharing these examples with you because at every youth game I coach, I notice most parents are distracted by their phones and often miss a lot of what is going on. Yes, they are at the game in physical form to support their children, but they are not there in mental form—they are in another world. Keep this in mind whenever or wherever you are with your kids. If you are in the same room as them or you are in the bleachers at one of their games and you are constantly going back and forth from the task at hand to your phone, you aren't really there. Your children will pick up on this. It sets a bad example and also teaches them that it is ok to do the same.

CHAPTER 7

Handheld Devices: How They Impact Emotional Development

Emotional Intelligence (EQ) is the ability to use, understand, and manage emotions in a productive, healthy way. It is what helps us communicate effectively, empathize with others, and overcome life's challenges. Studies have shown that people with high EQs have better mental and physical health, build stronger relationships, and perform better at their jobs. Studies have also shown that a high EQ matters twice as much in terms of superior leadership as IQ does. Unfortunately, emotional intelligence is not something that is taught in the classroom the way that English or history is, but it just may be the most fundamental skill for success.

Daniel Goleman, Ph.D., a well-known psychologist, created something known as the "mixed model" for emotional intelligence, which has five key areas:

1. Self-Awareness: Self-awareness involves knowing your own feelings. It involves knowing what your emotional triggers are and how you are going to deal with them when they occur.

2. Self-Management: Self-management involves keeping the emotions in check when they become disruptive. An example would be the ability to control outbursts or talk calmly with someone during a disagreement.

3. Motivation: The majority of people are motivated by outside things like money or other luxuries. According to Goleman, emotionally intelligent people are intrinsically motivated. They know that the outside stuff cannot provide joy and

happiness, so that does not motivate them. They are motivated for the sake of pure joy or being productive.

4. Empathy: The first three categories deal with handling one's own emotions, while empathy is the ability to support the emotions of someone else. It is the skill of reading another person's emotions and responding appropriately.

5. Social Skills: This is the ability to deal with others. People with strong social skills can find common ground with others at work, school, or anywhere. It is the ability to be persuasive.[38]

Obviously, we all want our children to possess these important skills, but there is a problem: most twenty-first-century children don't. This is why the phone at my private counseling practice is ringing like never before and why there are so many students having emotional meltdowns at my high school. It is also why colleges across the country are seeing double the number of emergency calls to their counseling departments. According to a September 2015 article in *Psychology Today written by* Peter Gray, a research professor at Boston College, students are having emotional crises and are seeking help for the minor problems of everyday life. One student who was upset about being called a "bitch" and another student who saw a mouse in her apartment sought counseling for trauma.[39]

According to Gray, faculty at colleges all across America noted that students' emotional fragility has become a serious problem when it comes to grading. Some professors have admitted that they are afraid to give low grades for poor performance because of the resulting student meltdowns they would have to deal with in their offices. Heads of counseling at a group of universities met several times to discuss the lack of student resilience that they were experiencing on their campuses. What the heads were experiencing was no different than what was being reported across the country on the state of late adolescence and early adulthood. Gray summarized some of the themes that emerged in the series of meetings, including the following:

- Students are needier and less resilient, leading faculty to have to do more handholding, lower their academic standards, and not challenge students too much.

- There is a sense of helplessness among the faculty. Many faculty members expressed their frustration with the current situation. There were few ideas about what institutions could do to address the issue.

- Students are afraid to fail; they do not take risks; they need to be certain about things. For many of them, failure is seen as catastrophic and unacceptable. External measures of success are more important than learning and autonomous development.

- Faculty, particularly young faculty members, feel pressured to accede to student wishes lest they get low teaching ratings from their students. Students email about trivial things and expect prompt replies.

- Failure and struggle need to be normalized. Students are very uncomfortable about not being right. They want to re-do papers to undo their earlier mistakes. Colleges have to normalize being wrong and learning from one's errors.

Do students who spend hours and hours using social media and technology fit into this dilemma? I believe they do. Remember the multitasking research conducted by Clifford Nass that we discussed earlier? Well, it turns out that the same area of the brain that is affected by multitasking is also the area that is responsible for managing emotions. According to Nass, "A strong emotional intelligence equals a healthy cerebral cortex, the frontal part of the brain that is responsible for executive functions."[40] When a message comes to the brain, the first thing it does is go to the emotional center of the brain, the area known as the amygdala. A brain that is working effectively will send that message to the cerebral cortex, which decides what to do with the information. People with low emotional intelligence have a weak connection between the emotional part of the brain (the amygdala) and the thinking part of the brain (the cerebral cortex). This weak connection leads to a host of different issues like social anxiety, general anxiety, and depression. What are the causes of this weak connection?

As I mentioned earlier, EQ is the ability to understand the emotions of others as well as the ability to understand and regulate one's own emotions. It is not something we are born with. It is something that can only be learned through observing voices, body posture, and facial expressions. In other words, it can only be learned and developed through face-to-face interaction with other people, not screen-to-screen interactions. The learning starts when we are young and, according to Nass, it turns out that it is hard. It was easier for previous generations to develop strong EQs because communicating face-to-face was all they had. There was nothing else to do. They couldn't pull out a smartphone or tablet to fill their downtime or communicate with one another. Bottom line, if you are distracted, you can't learn, and that includes learning emotions and learning proper human communication.

Another study tracked 3,400 tween girls (ages eight to twelve), which is the most critical time of development. The study looked at media use, face-to-face communication, and multitasking. Specific questions were asked with regard to social and emotional development. Those girls who used media while socializing with friends showed the following:

- Fewer feelings of being normal

- Greater feeling of peer pressure

- More friends who were bad influences

- Less sleep

Heavy online media use was also associated with negative social and emotional traits. There was, however, one variable in the study that had a positive predictor of social and emotional development, and it was the amount of face-to-face interaction one had.[41] What is the formula for a strong EQ? More face-to-face communication.

The sharp decrease in emotional intelligence we are seeing isn't just occurring on college campuses, it's happening at every educational level. As a public high school counselor for twenty-two years, I can tell you that the number and severity of mental and emotional health issues we are fielding is off the charts. I always tell folks that I wish they could shadow me for a day at the high school or at my private counseling practice. Although the majority of students are functioning well, there are an alarming number who are not. And, yes, there is one commonality between them: they are all highly immersed in their electronic and social media world. I could fill an entire book with examples, but I'll just give you a few.

SOCIAL SKILLS

A couple of years ago I attended a very nice ceremony for my son, who was bridging from Cub Scouts to Boy Scouts. There were a lot of parents there whom I knew quite well. One particular couple, Christine and Sanj, both cardiologists, were sitting at my table. Christine and I struck up a conversation about the millennial generation and the communication problems we were seeing. Christine works at a university hospital and told me a story about a recent medical school graduate she had interviewed for a residency. The candidate entered her office, took a seat, and crossed her arms. According to Christine, the candidate looked like she would rather have been watching paint dry than participate in this important interview. As Christine asked her questions, the candidate fidgeted in frustration and delivered her answers in an abrupt manner. Finally, the candidate asked Christine in a discourteous way, "Why are you asking me these questions?" Christine dismissed the candidate and received a very rude, self-absorbed email from her afterwards. You would think that someone who is smart enough to make it through medical school would have the communication skills that are necessary to do well at an interview. This young lady clearly did not have a strong enough emotional intelligence.

The counselor from the other high school in my school district and I have run a peer leadership program for many years. During trainings, students are paired with another student from their school. At a recent training, my colleague was short a student and I was able to lend him one of mine. When I introduced the two students to each other, there was an awkward silence. Both were really great kids but did not know what to say to each other; there was no instinctive introduction like, "Hello, my name is Jan." It wasn't the typical shyness you would expect from two fifteen-year-olds; it was outside of the norm. I couldn't help but wonder if their inability to connect with one another was because they've had little one-on-one, face-to-face contact in their lives. Has this once natural communication skill been sabotaged by text-to-text interaction?

I believe that our younger generation is not developing the critical communication skills that are required to ace a job interview or to simply meet someone new for the first time. As I mentioned in chapter 1 when we talked about neuroplasticity, if you don't use a skill you lose the skill. The example of the two students is one of many. I witness this underdeveloped communication set every day in my profession. After all, as a therapist and counselor, talking to people face-to-face is what I do. Colleagues of mine who are executives are seeing the same thing. They receive stellar resumes from recent college graduates, and when they bring them in for an interview there is something missing. There is a flatness in many of the candidates, a lack of eye-to-eye transference, and a void of confidence.

We need to engage our younger generation, our own children, face-to-face on a daily basis so that they can develop these important skills. We must push our children and their friends to be mentally and physically present with one another. That means that if your child has a friend over, limit the time spent in front of screens and increase the time spent playing and talking. The more they are exposed to this type of interaction, the stronger their communication skills and emotional intelligence will become.

PART THREE

What Parents Can Do: Tips, Techniques, and Solutions

CHAPTER 8

Raising Our Children to Be Leaders Instead of Followers

There are typically between one hundred and two hundred parents in attendance at my lectures. Since I am a funny guy (wink wink), I like to add humor, so I ask for a lot of audience participation. For example, I tell the audience, "Please raise your hand if you think it is appropriate for your middle school child to have M-rated video games such as Call of Duty or Grand Theft Auto." As expected, not a single hand goes up; all agree this is a terrible idea. Next, I tell them, "Please raise your hand if your child has one of these games." Again, not a single hand is raised, but I notice a lot of fidgeting and uncomfortable body language. Then I say, "Ok, so everyone agrees that M-rated games are not good for children under eighteen and no one in this room allows their child to have them. But the statistical truth is that more than half of you in attendance allow your children to play and own these games. In fact, it is you who purchased these games for your child. So more than half of you in the room are not being honest." I try not to put anyone on the spot or make anyone feel uncomfortable. Rather, this dialogue leads me to a discussion about something called social conformity.

Conformity is a type of social influence involving a change in belief or behavior in order to fit in with a group. For example, let's say your son is a fourth grader, around ten years old. You have always told him that he is not allowed to play M-rated video games until he is eighteen, and you were firm about this because you are a responsible parent. Then Christmas comes and one of your son's good friends gets Call of Duty as a gift. Before long, all of your son's friends get the game. You start to feel bad for your son because he is the only one whose parents won't break the rules and allow him to have this game. You go back and forth in your mind trying to figure out what you should do. Finally, you say to yourself, "You know what, every other kid has the game; the boys are now twelve, and they are a little more mature. If all of the other parents are ok with it, I guess it must not be that big of a deal. Plus, I want him to fit in, I don't want him to feel left out, and I certainly don't want him to get picked on for being the only kid who is not allowed to have these games. What the heck, he's doing well in school and he's responsible—I guess it's not a big deal." You get your son Call of Duty for his birthday.

This is a classic example of social conformity or peer pressure. And yes, it happens to us adults. The problem with this kind of adult peer pressure, this conformity, is that our children learn from us; they model our behavior. When we give in, we teach them to give in. When we ensure that they fit in with everyone else, that they follow suit, we are unintentionally teaching them how to be good followers instead of strong leaders.

A common fear that many of us share is that our children will not fit in. And in most cases that's exactly what it is—a fear, not a reality. Sometimes we go to the ends of the earth to make sure our children are included in every activity so that they don't become irrelevant. I witness this all the time in my community with sports, clothing, and electronic devices. We see what everyone else is doing and our minds tell us that must be the way to go. Without realizing it, we allow the collective group to make our decisions for us instead of deciding for ourselves what is right for our child. I believe this is why so many younger children now own smartphones. Although they make our lives easier when we need to get in touch with our children, I believe the risks are too great. The best bit of advice I can give you is to follow your parental instincts and be aware of trends going on around you. If your parental instinct is to tell your child, "Sorry, just because your friends have smartphones doesn't mean that you should have one," then go with that instinct. It will be a strong message.

Perhaps the most important message I'm trying to convey is that we don't want to teach our children to be followers of the crowd, we want them to be leaders. When we allow our children to have something that we know they are not mature enough to handle, for the sake of fitting in, we are teaching our children to follow the crowd.

It is our job as parents to do what is right for our children, not to allow outside influences to decide that for us. When I have these conversations with parents they sometimes become defensive because, let's face it, no adult wants to admit that they were peer pressured into anything.

A common reaction I get from parents who attend my lectures is that if their child didn't have a smartphone with texting and social media, then their child would have no friends because that is how kids communicate today. I understand this rationale and admit that I worried about this too at times, but now that my son is thirteen I can tell you this was an irrational worry. Even though my son does not text or use social media of any kind, he is constantly running around the street with friends, going to birthday parties, and simply enjoying being a boy. The things he's missing are the things I want him to be missing: gossip, inappropriate posts, and a potentially weakened sense of self. Ignorance is bliss! In fact, I was talking about this with a friend of mine recently and I told him that if I were to get my son a smartphone, I could say goodbye to his hard work in school, his dedication to sports, and his Eagle Scout aspirations, as he would become too distracted by superficial stuff. This is not a trade I am willing to make.

So what is the right age to get your child a smartphone? The best answer to this question is an answer that I once heard and it goes like this: *When you feel comfortable with your child watching pornography.* I don't think there is a better way to answer this because if you believe for a second that your child isn't going to click on the provocative images that pop up on a social media site, you've got another thing coming. And when they do click on that image, which they will, it will take them to places that no parent would want their child to go. Are you willing to make that sacrifice? I understand that children have laptops and tablets, where inappropriate content can also be accessed, but at least these devices are easier to manage. Smartphones are in their pockets and go with them wherever they go, making it much more difficult for us to regulate.

Mark Little, founder and president of Diversified Funding, a leading financial services firm, said it best: "A leader is someone [who] leads by example and has the integrity to do the right thing even when it is not popular. A good leader has positive influence over others, inspiring them to become a better person and example for others to model their life against, as well." Our children should memorize this quote and program it into their minds. Kids who have been taught to do what is right and follow the rules become intrinsically guided by their inner character and integrity. Being popular is not on their radar. Their confidence and character are such that even if a peer were to make fun of them for not being part of the social norm, it would be no sweat off their back; leaders have no face to save and nothing to prove to anyone but themselves. As parents, we are the only ones that can cultivate character and leadership in our children.

Let's go over some things you can do right now to make sure that you are not following the crowd and teaching your son or daughter to do the same.

- Never do what everyone else does simply because everyone else is doing it.

- Always listen to your gut instinct. If your gut tells you not to allow your son or daughter to visit a certain website or play a particular game, then don't allow it.

- If you fear that your children will fade into irrelevancy and you strive to ensure they fit in with everyone else, you are teaching them to be ordinary. Teach uniqueness and let your children grow from that.

- Your child will nag you for certain things, so stay firm; don't give in.

CHAPTER 9

Fragile Kids: The Media's Impact and What We Can Do about It

In October of 2012 there were a rash of kidnapping attempts throughout my community. Almost daily there was a story of another attempted luring plastered on the cover of every local and regional newspaper. It became the hot topic for the local television news stations too, and everyone's Facebook feeds were blowing up with this frightening news. Everyone around town was talking about the kidnappings, whether at church, the ball field, or at school. Everyone was on edge. After the nineteenth kidnapping attempt over the span of three weeks, I received a call from a local newspaper reporter asking for my professional insight and advice on this frightening situation. The reporter was stunned by my response because I told her that I didn't think a kidnapper existed. I said to her, "You mean to tell me that this alleged 'kidnapper' has failed all nineteen times in his attempt to abduct a child?" Then I gave my version of what I believed was happening. It looked something like this.

Ms. Reporter, what I believe has happened is that the first "luring attempt" probably wasn't a luring attempt at all. It was likely a couple of high school boys driving down a street who saw a younger child walking home from school, and they decided to do what many irrational teenagers do, pull a prank. Because teenage boys will be teenage boys, they thought it would be humorous to pull their car near the young child and say something like, "Hey, little girl, want some candy?" With that, the well versed youngster surely sprinted home as fast as she could to tell her mom what had happened because, like every other little girl or boy in the world, her parents had taught her to do that. Most certainly, the first thing the girl's mother did was call the police. And the second thing she did? See if you can guess . . . That's right, she immediately alerted all of her friends on Facebook. **Can you see the pandemonium unfolding?**

Within minutes, all of the other Facebook moms reposted this RED ALERT message to their friends and it immediately spread like wildfire. There is now a kidnapper lurking in our community. Every mom and dad would panic and their fear would be quickly projected upon their children. Every child in the community is on edge, and they're all talking about it at school. School administrators and teachers are notified and must come up with a plan. They hold an emergency meeting with students the following morning, advising them not to talk to strangers and to be alert. The anxiety among the kids goes viral.

Over the ensuing days, a child stops at the local candy store after school for a treat and notices a "strange-looking man" parked in the lot. The man signals to the child, perhaps asking for directions because he is lost, but the paranoid child doesn't see it that way; instead he panics. He runs home to tell his mom that "the kidnapper" tried to abduct him. Now kidnapping attempt number two has occurred, Facebook feeds light up even more, and the local news salivates. This continues for the next few weeks and by then there have been nineteen "attempted abductions" in the area, and countless children and adults are freaking out. Do you see the picture?

When I hung up the phone with the reporter I was certain she would not use my comments and I was fine with that. But my version of the kidnappings was right because the following day the great state of New Jersey, my state, was hit with the biggest hurricane in its history, Hurricane Sandy. Thousands of people lost their homes. Millions more lost power for days or weeks. There was chaos throughout the state, and the story lit up the news stations. Hurricane Sandy had taken over the television screens, computer screens, social media, and the newspapers. The "kidnapper" had mysteriously disappeared and not another word was ever mentioned about him. Perhaps he was blown away by the fierce winds of Hurricane Sandy.

Folks, we are living in fear and we are projecting this fear upon our children. Times have changed. With the incredible reach that digital and social media has, a breaking news story from the other side of the country will appear on your computer or smartphone screen within seconds. Ten or twenty years ago, we did not have this capability, so if there was a kidnapping in rural Mississippi we didn't know about it, let alone have the story transmitted to our suggestible brains over and over again, triggering our innate fear response.

Our society has changed so drastically because there is just *too much information*. Games like dodge ball and tag have been banned from school playgrounds because some parent decided to sue the school after their child sprained an ankle or suffered "emotional" harm because he or she wasn't very good at dodge ball. Then suddenly a story like this goes viral on social media, hits the TV screens and *bam*, bye-bye tag. Bye-bye dodge ball. Bye-bye being a kid. I've even done debates on television on such topics. One example was a segment I did on Fox News entitled "The Wussification of Schools." You can go to my YouTube channel to see it or follow this link: http://bit.ly/2fdAJ4F. The segment included three outrageous examples of how our children are being overprotected:

1. A parent of a college freshman sued the basketball coach and the school because his son did not get enough playing time senior year in high school, and the parent claims that they lost out on scholarship money because of it.

2. A school district banned "unsupervised cartwheels" during recess after a girl sprained her ankle.

3. A liberal arts college in New England banned "booing" at sporting events.

The reason we hear about stories like this is because of the incredible reach that digital media has, which can prompt other people and school personnel to establish similar, extraordinary rules. Just look at the countless schools across the country that have banned kids from playing the harmless game of tag. It starts with one headline story that goes viral and becomes contagious.

At a recent lecture, I shared with the audience that my son and daughter did not have cell phones and were perfectly fine without them. I explained that I did not want my kids' brains bombarded with drama, crazy stories, and other mind-altering content ; I just wanted them to be kids. One surprised parent asked me how I live not knowing what my kids were doing or where they were. She asked me, "What if there is an emergency?" You see, we have become so dependent on these devices that they now act as the umbilical cord that keeps our children within arm's reach all the time, and it's not healthy. How can we expect our children to detach from us, spread their wings, and make it as adults if the underlying message that we send to them is that the world is a dangerous place?

Other parents at my lectures have a different take. I will tell stories of students who are distracted all day long, during class, by their cell-phones, and some parents will ask, "Then why doesn't the school just ban them from being in the building?" Unfortunately, this is much easier said than done.

Cell phones entering schools often have very little to do with the school. If a school superintendent were to send home a letter telling parents in a school district that students were no longer allowed to bring these devices to school, the school would potentially be hit with lawsuits because many parents couldn't fathom not being able to get in contact with their child at a moment's notice. In many ways I understand this because of the mass tragedies like those in

Columbine and Newtown, Connecticut, but it runs deeper than this. Often times when I call a student out of class whom I need to speak with, they will receive text messages from their mom or dad. Keep in mind that their parents don't know their child is with me; they think he or she is in math or English class, yet they still send their children text messages. Ultimately, cellphones have become too convenient for us, and we have become accustomed to being able to reach out to our children and others at a moment's notice. We have become an instant gratification nation, and in many ways this is not a good thing.

THE iCONNECTED PARENT

In 2011, a book written by Middlebury College professor Barbara Hofer revealed the shocking truth about the overly connected parent/college student relationship. According to Hofer, until recently students handled college on their own, learning life's lessons, and they grew up in the process. Now students turn to their parents for answers to everything, rendering many of them incapable of learning how to handle life's fundamental challenges, like how to turn on the washing machine. Some parents are so protective of their kids that there are even stories of parents showing up to give professors a piece of their mind and trying to bail their kids out of everything. Hofer calls these the "iConnected parents," and her advice to them is this: just let go.[42] But in today's speed-dial, text-driven world, electronic devices have become the never-ending umbilical cord between parent and child—even adult, college-going children.

In an essay which appeared in the September, 2015 issue of *The Atlantic* magazine, Greg Lukianoff and Jonathan Haidt describe a related phenomenon that is happening in American colleges and universities. According to the authors, "A movement is arising, driven mostly by students, to scrub campuses clean of words, ideas and subjects that might cause discomfort and give offense." Professors around the country find themselves having to teach in a more gingerly fashion for fear of a strong emotional response that some of the academic content might trigger in some of their students. The student movement is about emotional well-being and presumes an extraordinary fragility in the collegiate psyche, and therefore elevates the goal of protecting students from psychological harm. And it does appear that this generation of college students is suffering from more mental health issues than previous generations. In a 2013 survey, college mental health directors reported an across-the-board increase in the number of students with severe psychological problems. [43] It seems that the ultimate aim of this student movement, according to Lukianoff and Haidt, is to turn campuses into "safe spaces" where young adults are shielded from words and ideas that make some uncomfortable. And this movement seeks to punish anyone who interferes with that aim, even accidentally. The authors call this impulse *vindictive protectiveness*. It is creating a culture in which everyone must think twice before speaking up, lest they face charges of insensitivity, aggression, or worse. As Lukianoff and Haidt sum up the current situation, "Students seem to be reporting more emotional crises; many seem fragile, and this has surely changed the way university faculty and administrators interact with them. The question is whether some of those changes might be doing more harm than good."[44]

In conclusion, our devices have become such a part of who we are that we may be losing sight of who we are. We have learned to crave the endless streams of information and communication pouring from all forms of digital media. If we want an immediate answer to something, we turn to our phone. If we need to remind our children of something or contact them, we cannot delay—we must do it now. Much of the social media and news content that we are on the receiving end of is nonstop and gets into our heads, often leading to fear, worry, and anxiety. The only way to protect our brains and the brains of our children is to become self-aware about our incessant digital communications and to make a commitment to start delaying our need for instant gratification. We must become more patient and less impulsive.

CHAPTER 10

Using Mindfulness and Meditation to Reconnect Our Disconnected Kids

Now that you understand how technology may be affecting your child, it's time to come up with some strategies to solve this problem. Let's begin with five rules that every parent should follow.

1. **Keep your child's room clean of screens:** Your child should never have any type of electronic device in his room, period. This includes televisions, computers, and handheld devices. If your child tends to do homework in his bedroom and claims that he will need his computer to do it, have him do it in the family room. No matter how much grief you get, remember that you are in charge. Keep those screens *out* of the bedroom.

2. **Your child's phone is your phone:** Your child's phone is yours, not hers. Make this very clear to her and have a rule that the phone is to be handed to you at a certain time every night. Your child should never be allowed to sleep with the phone next to her. That is a recipe for disaster as the temptation to communicate via text and social media will be too strong, thereby creating sleep disturbances and other issues.

3. **No electronics during dinner:** Make a rule that dinnertime is family time. No phones or televisions can be used during this important time, by anyone—including you. Make dinnertime sacred.

4. **Limit screen time for entertainment purposes (including TV) to two hours per day:** Yes, I get it. This sounds like an

impossible task, but this is what the Academy of American Pediatrics recommended for children over eight years of age before they lightened their guidelines. But I still agree with the old ones.

5. **Be a role model:** This means spending less time with your beloved device when you are with your children. Turn off your device during dinner and whenever you are in the presence of your children. Our children need us to be present when we are around them, not distracted.

Stick to these tips and you will be well on your way to gaining control of technology in your home. Now it's time to get into some of the deeper strategies that will help you and your child to be in control of technology instead of being controlled by it.

STEPPING INTO THE UNKNOWN: THE REAL WORLD

There is no textbook answer to solving the problem that all of this technology is bestowing upon our families. In a perfect world, the answer would look something like this: *Just get rid of the computer, smartphones, and video games.* This is obviously unrealistic. Technology is here to stay, but there are plenty of strategies that you can introduce to your family to ensure that your children develop into fine men and women. It starts with introducing them to a new way of thinking, a new type of awareness. Let me explain.

Technology addiction, like drug addiction, strips children of their identity; they can lose sight of who they are, their sense of self. Rather than thinking for themselves, they will become controlled by their thoughts. Most children have never met the person who lies deep within because they have become hypnotized by machines and have not developed a connection to their inner being. But I intend to help you change this. It is important that we introduce our children to someone they barely know—themselves. The only way to do this is to teach them some simple mind strategies, which I will get to shortly. First, let me give you a crash course on mindfulness.

Our mind is the result of the millions of impressions we have received from home, work, school, friends, and everything else we encounter. Nearly all of our life experiences—the things we've seen and heard, including from social media and television—are accepted by the subconscious with little or no inspection. The conscious mind receives the information and then passes it along to the subconscious, and this information is built into us mentally, emotionally, and physically. We become our thoughts. What we are today is a result of our past thinking and our past experiences. And what we become tomorrow will be the result of how we think today. It is our job to ensure that our children's minds are receiving large doses of healthy, genuine stimuli as opposed to superficial cyber-stimuli.

Look at it like this: if you were planting a garden, you'd be careful to do it right. You'd buy the best soil, the best seeds, and the best sprinkler system, and you'd care for that garden so that you could grow the best crop. But when it comes to our children's mental gardens, we can become careless. Their mental garden is more important than anything else because whatever enters into their life depends on the quality of the seeds planted in their minds and how those seeds are cared for. Let's face it: if the seeds sown by social media and technology consist of gossip, fear, and a drive to keep up with the Jones's, our children's mental crop will become weak and decayed. If seeds of courage, optimism, and hope are planted, cared for, and nurtured, and these thoughts refuse to associate with any damaging thoughts received from other sources, then your child's mental garden will be bountiful.

Our children have been taught their whole lives to look everywhere else but inside of themselves for answers. Without intending to, they have exposed themselves to far too many negative things because of electronic media, facilitating a mindset of lack, fear, and worry. They don't know any better because they live in a world where they are constantly connected to a device, causing them to become disconnected from their inner selves. It is our job to protect their impressionable minds. Teaching our children how to turn inward will help them to become self-secure because they can focus on their talents, desires, and dreams. Let's talk about how we can do this.

WALKING WITH A LIGHTER STEP

Regardless of the problems that clients come to me with, they all have the same thing in common—their thoughts are controlling them rather than the other way around. I developed an effective strategy to help my clients take control of their thoughts and therefore their lives. I call it *walking with a lighter step* and it is something you can learn and your children can learn. Here's how it works.

My office suite is located on the second floor of an office building that faces the rear parking lot. During my initial session with clients I ask them if they know where their car is parked. I then ask them to point it out to me from my office window. Then I ask how long they think it would take for them to walk to their car from my office. The answer for each person is always a little different. Some will say, "A minute." Others will say, "Forty seconds." Others might say, "Two minutes." Next, I ask this: "Let's assume that when you return for your session next week, you park in that exact same spot. How long do you think it would take you next week to walk to your car after our session has ended?" The answer is always the same as their first response. If a client said thirty seconds, they would say thirty seconds again. I then ask, "Why is this? Why wouldn't it take a little longer or a little faster to walk to the car?" Their response is usually along the lines of "I don't know; because my stride is always the same" or "because I'm a fast walker."

The purpose of this metaphor is to point out to them that nearly everything we do throughout the day is habitual, automatic. We shower the same way. We eat our meals the same way, and we drive our cars the same way, to name just a few activities. If you eat right-handed, you're not suddenly going to eat left-handed. If you are a fast chewer of your food, you're not suddenly going to start chewing slowly. Ultimately, most of what we do all day long is unconscious, meaning we don't have to "think" about what we are doing. Something as simple as walking, whether it's to the car or to a neighbor's house, is unconscious; you don't have to think about it to do it, like riding a bike. After your brain has learned how to do something, you no longer have to try—it just happens.

I would bet that if you timed yourself while taking a shower that your time would be within seconds of the previous time. The mind is a supercomputer and once new learning is programmed into it, the brain switches to autopilot. This may sound like a good thing, and in some ways it is, but it is also the cause of many of our problems. Here's why.

The more we go about our day "mindlessly" controlled by the unconscious, the less control we have consciously. An inner dialogue occurs during our unconscious moments, a self-talk that is unrelated to whatever mindless task we are engaged in, whether it's walking to the car or driving the car. The mind is always wandering. It is called daydreaming, and often our daydreaming thoughts are filled with insecurities and fears, especially for children. They worry about friends, school, and what others think of them, and they don't realize they are doing this. The thoughts orbiting around in their subconscious universe all day long may not be positive, and the deluge of information and images coming from social media and technology don't help.

It's been stated that we have approximately sixty thousand thoughts a day, most of which come from this daydreaming, subconscious mind.[45] When these daydreaming thoughts are littered with worry, fear, and self-doubt, you can be sure that your life will not be as desired. Changing those subconscious daydreams requires help from the conscious, "present" mind. When we focus on being mentally "present," we gain control of our thoughts, our body, and our emotions. Feeling our feet hitting the floor as we walk or the breath of air we are taking means that we are present and self-aware. It is from this "present" place that we can begin to take control of the daydreaming thoughts that sabotage us.

When I ask my clients what they would need to do in order for it to take them thirty seconds longer to walk to their car from my office, the answer is usually "walk more slowly" or "take my time." This is true, but there is something that has to happen first before they take that first, slower step. That's right: they have to catch themselves and *think* about walking more slowly. In other words, they have to become conscious. This type of conscious presence is the key to solving just about all of our problems. These present-moment awakenings, or "intentional" thoughts, remove us from the often dark clouds of the subconscious, allowing us to be in command of our thoughts and therefore our feelings. Anytime we "stop and think" or "smell the roses," we are in a creative state because we get to paint whatever picture we want in our imagination. We can think about what we are grateful for. We can think about what we want to accomplish in life. We can think about how it feels to be motivated and confident, and so on. The more we practice "present-moment" thinking, the sooner our subconscious will improve. Those sixty thousand drifting thoughts per day will begin to change, and they will begin to serve us. The more we become masters of the conscious and present mind, the stronger the subconscious gets.

Imagine you and your child going about your day and remembering as many times as you can to become mindfully present. Imagine you are at your desk, in the kitchen, or in your car and catching yourself in the present moment, and expanding on that present moment. Maybe you are thinking about your wonderful home and family or maybe about being promoted or losing weight, or whatever. With practice, you and your children become in control of your thoughts and ultimately your outcomes.

Our thoughts become things. When we feed the mind with thoughts of success, abundance, and confidence, eventually those thoughts make their way into the hard drive of our mind, the subconscious. And remember, it is the subconscious mind that controls about 95 percent of every aspect of us. Those sixty thousand thoughts you have every day will work in your favor. As you and your children begin to master this mindfulness strategy, you will soon be ready to apply some even more powerful strategies to help gain back control of the mind, body, and emotions.

MINDFULNESS AND TECHNOLOGY

You might be wondering what all of this mindfulness stuff has to do with our children's obsession with technology? Think back to your childhood for a moment. Remember those rainy days in the summer when you paced around the house trying to figure out what to do? Yes, that feeling of boredom. Well, boredom is to your brain what weight lifting is to your muscles. That's right: boredom is the mental fertilizer that the mind so desperately needs. Sadly, it is something that most children have never experienced.

Ask any child if she has ever sat in complete silence and paid attention to her thoughts simply because there was nothing else to do. You will find few. Kids today have no idea what boredom is because there is always an electronic device on hand to occupy them, to distract them from their boredom. Unfortunately, the very thing they are distracting themselves from—their thoughts—is the thing they need the most in order to thrive and succeed.

Earlier, I mentioned that there's an even faster way to start reprogramming the mind. It's called meditating. Meditation may sound clichéd, but look at it a bit differently—as a way of escaping from the distractions of technology, and a way to focus your thinking. All it takes is five or ten minutes a day of your time. Start doing it for yourself first and then introduce it to your children. Here's a quick beginner exercise. You can also go to my website and receive an audio version of the exercise by clicking here: http://tomkersting.com/.

Find a quiet place, **every day,** *where you can sit in total silence completely free from all distractions, including electronic devices. Start by forming an image of something in your mind, something simple like a flower. Color that flower any color you wish. Shape the flower any way you choose. After doing this every day for a week, move on to something else that suits you, like an image of a goal that you have. For your children, maybe the image is succeeding in school or feeling determined. Make sure you breathe deeply as you do this and stay focused on the image you have created. Remind your child to do the same. This is* *particularly helpful if your child has anxiety. He or she can focus on an image of calmness and confidence. The more this is practiced, the sooner it takes root in the subconscious mind, which is the part of the mind that is creating how we feel all the time.*

More important than the images that you or your child create while practicing this simple technique is the mental creativeness that will begin to develop, naturally. This inner world is what I call the bottom of the iceberg and the outer world the tip. If your children practice these mental time-outs with great regularity, they will discover that reality and personal abundance exist in the inside world, not their outer, gadget-filled world. You and your children will start to feel mentally wiser, emotionally stronger, and more relaxed.

THE POWER OF CONCENTRATION

Concentration is an important part of connecting to the inner self. For children this can be very difficult because any opportunities for downtime are usually replaced with tablets and smartphones, reducing their ability to be in control of their thinking. The art of concentration is the ability to steer the mind and shape our thoughts. Doing this correctly will strengthen your child's mind and emotions.

Have your child practice this simple concentration exercise:

Choose a specific vacation destination that you've enjoyed in the past. For five minutes, close your eyes and focus all of your attention on that place—the details, the climate, the hotel, and the atmosphere. Everything.

Your child is going to find this difficult to do because his mind will wander off and think about things that have nothing to do with the vacation destination. And many of these wandering thoughts will be unpleasant. This is an example of how the mind can have control over us instead of us controlling it. The good news is that with regular practice your child will become a master at controlling and directing his or her thoughts.

Your child can use a similar concentration technique to help foster positive feelings. Here's how: have your child select a picture that represents a positive feeling she would like to have, such as happiness. Have her stare at the picture for a few minutes. I like to use a picture of Rocky Balboa from the movie *Rocky* because, to me, it represents determination. Have your child do the following:

Close your eyes after you've examined the picture for several minutes and try to see it vividly in your imagination. Try to see every detail. As in the first exercise, it will seem difficult to hold that picture in your thoughts for any length of time. Practice until you can see every detail for a full five minutes. Don't worry: you'll be able to do this.

Once your child has mastered this simple exercise, she will have learned the first most important step in controlling her thoughts—concentration. This is the starting point for learning how to control feelings and attitude.

Successful athletes regularly practice similar techniques. In fact, many studies have been conducted with athletes to see if they can succeed at their sport by practicing their routine only in their imagination. Olympic athletes, for example, have been hooked up to sophisticated biofeedback devices, demonstrating that the same muscles that fired while competing also fired when they imagined they were competing.[46] This is evidence that our thoughts have an impact on our body and emotions. Similar studies have been done with basketball players. One group of players was instructed to rehearse shooting free throws only in their imagination for a period of time, and the control group practiced shooting real free throws in their usual way. The group that imagined shooting free throws had the same success rate in games as the group who practiced shooting real free throws.[47] Amazing! As your child practices these simple mental exercises, he will begin to see changes in how he thinks and feels and acts.

UNDOING ANXIETY

A common link to disease is worry, also known as anxiety. Anxiety comes directly from the subconscious because the subconscious is like a sponge and absorbs all of the stimuli we are exposed to in the world—and there's an awful lot of it. Think about world news and all other forms of media and how we have unintentionally given our mind free reign to wander off and absorb these messages. That's exactly why our children's subconscious can become programmed with bad stuff. It's not much different than letting your four-year-old go on a shopping spree at a candy store; it will lead to disaster. This wandering off is something you experienced just a few moments ago when I asked you to do the simple task of focusing on a vacation destination.

The only way to destroy anxiety and other mental health disorders like depression is to gain mind control, and that requires focus. Getting into the cockpit and taking over the control panels of your mind is how it is done. And it's what our children must do in order to become healthy adults one day. As they learn to become mindful and apply these brief meditations, they will start to take control of their lives. Since this will likely be new to your child, it might seem a little complicated at first, but it isn't. It just requires practice. They will recreate themselves because they will be able to awaken their mind to the power within. It is imperative that you and your children practice this until you trust that the process works. I promise it will.

In her bestselling book, *The Secret*, Rhonda Byrne explains that in the 1700s when Benjamin Franklin was searching for electricity, no one believed it was possible because electricity could not be seen. She goes on to point out that although we can't see electricity, we know it exists.[48] How else can you explain this mysterious thing that lights our homes and powers our refrigerators? Electricity is real even though we can't see it, and we have 100 percent trust in its existence. There is no disputing this. Like electricity, you can't explain your existence but you know you are real. The flesh and blood part of you is just the host of the real *you*, also known as energy or spirit.

You must trust that *you* are real the same way you trust that electricity is real. This is a very important part of discovering the relationship that is the most important—the one with your *self*.

This energy or spirit that I describe is as real as electricity. And I'll even go a little further. It actually is electricity. If you were to place your hand under a proper microscope you would no longer see flesh and blood, you would see energy vibrating.

FAITH IN YOUR CHILD

Throughout time, every civilization has believed in an invisible power that is the cause of everything. Some call it God. Some call it energy. Some call it spirit. Regardless of your definition, the effect is the same. We may not be able to explain what makes grass grow or what makes a cut heal, but we know that there is a cause. We rely on our five senses to decide what is real or what isn't—but who is to say that there are only five senses? Maybe there are more. As St. Thomas Aquinas wrote, "To one who has faith, no explanation is necessary. To one without faith, no explanation is possible."

As a therapist and school counselor for twenty-two years, I've entered the lives of thousands of people and have developed a sixth sense. Within seconds of meeting someone, I can tell exactly what they are feeling before they utter a word. And often I can tell the person what he is thinking. I can do this because my work has allowed me to become attuned to other people's feelings. I can feel their energy. It's real. Would it make sense to ignore this skill and brush it off because I cannot see, hear, or smell it? Of course not! I use it to my advantage and, as a result, my clients can feel that I can intuit their feelings, which helps me help them. Don't believe for a minute that your powers are limited to the five senses. You are much greater than that and soon you will realize this.

Faith is defined as a confidence or trust in a person or entity. People use expressions such as "have faith that everything will work out" or "I have faith in you." What they're really saying is "wake up and focus on the things you want, not on the things you don't want." The vehicle that directs our faith is the mind. If your child thinks about success, health, and abundance, she will reap the rewards of those thoughts. If she thinks thoughts of poverty, disease, and despair, then she will get what she wished for. Our children need to develop the faith that they are supreme beings and that they are the composers of their thoughts. If they don't, they will never live up to their full potential.

In conclusion, our greatest gift is our ability to think. Unfortunately, many of us do not know how to do this correctly because we have relinquished this skill to modern technology. But it is not too late to change. Proper thinking is the path that leads to the inner self. The inner self holds all of the answers to helping us overcome virtually anything so that we can live our life to the fullest. The inner self is very real, and all of us have unlimited access to this world; we're just not aware of it. Those who are connected to this omnipotent place are invincible. They are positivity magnets, and everything they acquire in the "outside" world is a result of the work they have done inside. As you and your children practice mastering the inner self, you will all be able to balance the amount of technology in your lives and move on to greater happiness and fulfillment.

The quality of our children's lives is only as good as the relationship they have with their self, the inner self. Your children need to learn who they truly are; they are not some superficial number that is based on the number of "friends" or "likes" they have on social media. By applying proper mental strategies, they will discover this. And if you think you could never get your child to meditate, remember the words of Andrew Carnegie: "Whether you think you can or think you can't, either way you are right." So start thinking that you can. After all, wouldn't you do anything for your child? God bless! Happy unplugging!

ACKNOWLEDGEMENT

I would like to thank my beautiful wife and two wonderful children for all their support and encouragement in everything I do.

ABOUT THE AUTHOR

Tom Kersting is a nationally renowned psychotherapist, and school counselor. He appears regularly on the most popular talk shows and news shows and has hosted television series' and shows for A&E Network, National Geographic Channel, Food Network and Oprah's Wellness Network. He maintains a busy counseling practice in New Jersey.

If you want to receive an automatic email when Tom's next book is released, sign up here http://bit.ly/2fVdnhY. You will only be contacted when a new book is released and your email address will never be shared.

Word of mouth is extremely important for any author to succeed. If you enjoyed this book, it would be a great help if you left a brief review at Amazon by clicking here: http://amzn.to/2hqC07y.

SPEAKING

If you are interested in having Tom speak to your group or organization, please visit Tom's website at www.tomkersting.com.

Finally, I always love to hear your comments and feedback, so you're welcome to email me: tom@tomkersting.com. You can also tweet me @tomkersting or join my Facebook Page https://www.facebook.com/Thomas-Kersting-147086975353891/.

I often post motivational videos on my YouTube Channel so please feel free to visit: http://bit.ly/2gCB2Z7

NOTES

1. Gary Small, Teena D. Moody, Prabha Siddarth, and Susan Y. Bookheimer, "Your Brain on Google: Patterns of Cerebral Activation during Internet Searching," *American Journal of Geriatric Psychiatry* 17:2 (2009): 116–26.

2. Benny Evangelista, "Attention Loss Feared as High-Tech Rewires Brain," *San Francisco Chronicle*, November 15, 2009.

3. European College of Neuropsychopharmacology, press release, September 19, 2016.

4. Marion K. Underwood and Robert W. Faris, "#Being13: Inside the Secret World of Teens," CNN Special Report, October 2015, http://www.cnn.com/specials/us/being13.

5. Kevin P. Collins and Sean D. Cleary, "Racial and Ethnic Disparities in Parent-Reported Diagnosis of ADHD: National Survey of Children's Health (2003, 2007, and 2011), *Journal of Clinical Psychiatry* 77:1 (2016): 52–59.

6. All names and identifying details of clients have been changed to protect their privacy.

7. Victoria J. Rideout, Ulla G. Foehr, and Donald F. Roberts, "Generation M²: Media in the Lives of 8- to 18-Year-Olds," A Kaiser Family Foundation Study, January 2010.

8. Victoria J. Rideout, Ulla G. Foehr, and Donald F. Roberts, "Generation M²: Media in the Lives of 8- to 18-Year-Olds," A Kaiser Family Foundation Study, January 2010.

9. "Zero to Eight: Children's Media Use in America 2013," A Common Sense Media Research Study, October 2013.

10. Veronica Rocha, "2 California Med Fall Off Edge of Ocean Bluff while Playing 'Pokemon Go'," *Los Angeles Times*, July 14, 2016.

11. Kirstan Conley, "Many NYC Students So Teach-Oriented They Can't Even Sign Their Own Names," *New York Post*, January 27, 2016.

12. Haley Goldberg, "Your Smartphone Is Making You Hallucinate," *New York Post*, January 5, 2016.

13. Helena Horton, "Could You Get 'Selfie Stomach'? Internet Addict Develops Painful Disease from Hunching over Her Computer," *The Telegraph*, January 6, 2016.

14. Anthony Cuthbertson, "Smartphones Cause Drooping Jowls and 'Tech-Neck' Wrinkles in 18–39 Year-Olds," *International Business Times*, January 12, 2015.

15. Chris Weller, "Texting Puts 50 Pounds of Pressure on Your Spine, Adding to Poor Posture's Side Effects," *Medical Daily*, November 18, 2014.

16. Elisabeth Sherman, "Doctors Confirm That Cell Phones Cause Cancer," *All That Is Interesting*, May 4, 2016.

17. Marion K. Underwood and Robert W. Faris, "#Being13: Inside the Secret World of Teens," CNN Special Report, October 2015, http://www.cnn.com/specials/us/being13.

18. Susan Kelley, "'Likes' Less Likely to Affect Self-Esteem of People with Purpose," *Phys.Org*, September 21, 2016.

19. Sabrina Tavernise, "Young Adolescents as Likely to Die From Suicide as From Traffic Accidents," *New York Times*, November 3, 2016.

20. Rachel Simmons, *Odd Girl Out: The Hidden Culture of Aggression in Girls* (New York: Mariner Books, 2003).

21. Eyal Ophir, Clifford Nass, and Anthony D. Wagner, "Cognitive Control in Media Multitaskers," *Proceedings of the National Academy of Sciences of the United States of America* 106: 37 (2009), 15583–15587.

22. Sanjay Gupta, "Your Brain on Multitasking," CNN, http://www.cnn.com/2015/04/09/health/your-brain-multitasking

23. Gary Small, Teena D. Moody, Prabha Siddarth, and Susan Y. Bookheimer, "Your Brain on Google: Patterns of Cerebral Activation during Internet Searching," *American Journal of Geriatric Psychiatry* 17:2 (2009): 116–26.

24. Benny Evangelista, "Attention Loss Feared as High-Tech Rewires Brain," *San Francisco Chronicle*, November 15, 2009.

25. Travis Bradberry, "Multitasking Damages Your Brain and Your Career, New Studies Suggest," Talentsmart.com, accessed November 16, 2016, http://www.talentsmart.com/articles/Multitasking-Damages-Your-Brain-and-Your-Career,-New-Studies-Suggest-2102500909-p-1.html.

26. Jeff Guo, "Why Smart Kids Shouldn't Use Laptops in Class," *Washington Post*, May 2016.

27. James Doubek, "Attention, Students: Put Your Laptops Away," NPR Weekend Edition Sunday, April 17, 2016.

28. Common Sense Media, "Distraction, Multitasking and Time Management," 2014.

29. Tom Phillips, "Taiwan Orders Parents to Limit Children's Time with Electronic Games," *The Telegraph*, January 28, 2015.

30. Tom Phillips, "Chinese Teen Chops Hand off to 'Cure' Internet Addiction," February 3, 2015.

31. "Stories of Video Game Addiction," accessed November 16, 2016, http://www.video-game-addiction.org/stories-of-addiction.html.

32. "Global Report: US and China Take Half of $113BN Games Market in 2018," Newzoo, May 18, 2015.

33. John Raphael, "Study: How Videogame Addiction Affects Sleep Habits, Obesity, Cardio-Metabolic Health," *Nature World News*, May 11, 2016.

34. Norman Herr, "Television & Health," accessed November 16, 2016, http://www.csun.edu/science/health/docs/tv&health.html.

35. add link

36. "Technology Addiction: Concern, Controversy, and Finding Balance," Common Sense Media Research Report, May 2016.

37. Janet Morrissey, "Your Phone's on Lockdown. Enjoy the Show," *New York Times,* October 15, 2016.

38. "Emotional Intelligence: Mixed Model," Universal Class, accessed November 16, 2016, https://www.universalclass.com/articles/psychology/emotional-intelligence-mixed-model.htm.

39. Peter Gray, "Declining Student Resilience: A Serious Problem for Colleges," *Psychology Today*, September 22, 2105.

40. Clifford Nass, "Are You Multitasking Your Life Away?," TEDxStanford, https://www.youtube.com/watch?v=PriSFBu5CLs.

41. Roy Pea, Clifford Nass, *et al*, "Media Use, Face-to-Face Communication, Media Multitasking, and Social Well-Being among 8- 12-Year-Old Girls," *Developmental Psychology* 48:2 (2012): 327–336.

42. Barbara K. Hofer and Abigail Sullivan Moore, *The iConnected Parent: Staying Close to Your Kids in College (and Beyond) While Letting Them Grow Up* (New York: Atria Books, 2010).

43. Peter Gray, "Declining Student Resilience: A Serious Problem for Colleges," *Psychology Today*, September 22, 2105.

44. Greg Lukianoff and Jonathan Haidt, "The Coddling of the American Mind," *The Atlantic*, September 2015.

45. "Don't Believe Everything You Think," Cleveland Clinic Wellness, accessed November 16, 2016, http://bit.ly/2fXAd7S.

46. Ken Johnston, "The Olympics, Then . . . Now . . . and the Edge," Creating Positive Change, accessed November 16, 2016, http://freshairecreatingpositivechange.blogspot.com/2010/02/olympics-thennowand-edge.html

47. Joe Haefner, "Mental Rehearsal & Visualization: The Secret to Improving Your Game Without Touching a Basketball!," Breakthrough Basketball, accessed November 16, 2016, https://www.breakthroughbasketball.com/mental/visualization.html.

48. Rhonda Byrne, *The Secret* (New York: Atria Books, 2006).

Made in the USA
San Bernardino, CA
29 November 2017